EVERY PERSON'S
GUIDE TO
DEATH AND DYING
IN THE JEWISH TRADITION

EVERY PERSON'S
GUIDE TO
DEATH AND DYING
IN THE JEWISH TRADITION

RONALD H. ISAACS

JASON ARONSON INC.
Northvale, New Jersey
Jerusalem

This book was set in 12 pt. Weiss by Hightech Data Inc., of Bangalore, India and printed and bound by Book-mart Press, Inc. of North Bergen, NJ.

Library of Congress Cataloging-in-Publication Data

Isaacs, Ronald H.
    Every person's guide to death and dying in the Jewish tradition /
  by Ronald H. Isaacs.
      p. cm.
  Includes bibliographical references and index.
  ISBN 0–7657–6028–2
  1. Jewish mourning customs. 2. Funeral rites and ceremonies,
Jewish. 3. Death—Religious aspects—Judaism. I. Title.
BM712.I719 1998
296.4'45—dc21   98–15225

Printed in the United States of America. Jason Aronson Inc. offers books and cassettes. For information and catalog write to Jason Aronson Inc., 230 Livingston Street, Northvale, NJ 07647-1726, or visit our website: http://www.aronson.com

For
Norm VanArsdale

You turned my mourning into dancing.
—(Psalm 30)

CONTENTS

Contents

Introduction

The Jewish way of life, through specific rites and rituals, helps to order and structure our response to the experience of death. The Jewish way of death is different than the American way of death, just as the Jewish way of life is different. In Judaism, the rites and rituals are an attempt to face death realistically. For example, its insistence upon confronting death directly is reflected in the traditional requirement that the tearing of a mourner's garment (nowadays often using a symbolic black ribbon) as a sign of the tear in our hearts must be done while the mourner is standing.

The simplicity of a traditional Jewish burial, unlike in most other religions, is designed to avert and avoid ostentation. In Judaism, the democracy of death is evident by the dressing of the deceased in similar white linen shrouds, as a sign of purity. All are equal in death, no matter what their social or economic status.

The Jewish way of life and death also finds order and meaning through structure. Instead of letting death consume mourners, Judaism is able to transform bereavement into a vehicle with the potential to strengthen familial ties, revitalize communal solidarity, and promote the sanctity of life itself.

Judaism also prescribes an array of practices, rites, and rituals related to the observance of mourning and post-mourning practices (unveiling, *yizkor, yahrzeit*). It also posits a variety of beliefs related to the world beyond the grave, including the world to come, resurrection, reincarnation, and various views on the soul.

Every Person's Guide to Death and Dying in the Jewish Tradition is designed to present and walk the reader through the basic rites, beliefs, and practices related to the Jewish way of death and dying. Since Reform and Reconstructionist Judaism affords more free choice within the framework of Judaism and personal autonomy to follow that choice when it is made from a base of Jewish knowledge, this volume will also point out where these branches of Judaism may deviate from the Jewish traditional viewpoint.

Topics in this book will include: what Judaism says about life and death, the *mitzvah* of "kevod hamet" (honoring the dead), before death (visiting the sick, confession, and ethical wills), from death to bereavement, the funeral and burial, mourning observances, post-mourning observances, special questions and concerns (suicide, cremation, amputated limbs, and mausoleums).

In addition, the book will also feature quotations culled from the Bible, Talmud, and Midrash related to various topics on death and dying, a chapter on explaining death to children, a section of readings and comforting reflections related to the meaning of life and death, a glossary of terms, an appendix that includes prayers for visiting a cemetery, a guide to reading a tombstone, suggested *yizkor* remembrance prayers, and a bibliography with suggestions for further reading and study.

May this book help you to better understand the meaning of life and death and the sensitive way in which Jewish tradition relates to these issues. And may God always comfort you in your time of bereavement.

—Rabbi Ronald Isaacs

ONE

The Sanctity of Life and Death—The Jewish Perspective

*The dust returns to the earth as it was, but the spirit
returns to God who gave it.*
—(Ecclesiastes 3:2)

The Mishna Sanhedrin says that "Whoever saves one life, it is as if
that person saved the entire world." From Judaism's perspective, life
is a gift from God, and each human being is of supreme importance, having been created in God's image. The preservation of
human life takes precedence over every other consideration. This
includes the Jewish obligation to visit the sick and the permission
to violate the Sabbath to help a person afflicted with a dangerous
illness. It also includes, as will be described later in this book, the
obligation of forbearance from doing anything that might hasten
the death of a sick person, no matter how serious the illness.

Furthermore, it is the responsibility of every Jew to take care
of his or her body. Thus a whole body of rabbinic law has been
issued over the centuries related to proper diet, exercise, and the
like.

The sacredness of human life extends to both body and soul because both are the handiwork of God. Thus, just as there is a Jewish way of life, so too there is a Jewish way of death and dying. Over the centuries rabbinic thinkers have offered an array of practices and rituals which are concerned with every aspect of death. These practices gives expression both to respect and reverence for the dead as well as concern for the bereaved.

In America today, many persons who are dying often continue to be isolated in hospitals or nursing homes, treated as collections of organs and illnesses rather than as complete human beings. Our society continues to be a death-denying one, and many people avoid those for whom death is imminent.

When Rabbi Yochanan finished the book of Job he used to say: "The end of man is to die and the end of a beast is to be slaughtered, and all are doomed to die. It's a simple and undeniable as that."

There are several underlying principles that are fundamental to understanding the Jewish way of death and dying. Among these are:

REALITY

The laws of death and dying reflect a realistic view. Judaism has always insisted on confronting death directly. Already in biblical times, we are presented with numerous examples of Bible heroes facing death simply with honesty. "Behold, I am now about to go in the way of all the earth," (Kings 2:2) says David to his son, and "Behold, I am now about to die," says Jacob to Joseph (Genesis 48:21).

The need to prepare for death all of one's life and to know about it is a motif that pervades Jewish tradition. For example, on Yom Kippur, the day of atonement, Jewish custom is for the worshipper to dawn a *kittel* (white robe), symbol of freedom and purity. Similarly, the deceased is buried in a white linen shroud, thus reminding the worshipper that days pass by quickly and that one must always be prepared for one's own death.

Another example of realism is the section of prayers to be recited when dying that is found in the traditional prayerbook. Here is an excerpt from this section whose lines are honest while at the same time filled with optimism:

> I acknowledge before you, Adonai my God and God of my ancestors, that my life and death are in Your hands. May it be Your will to heal me. But if death is my lot, then I accept it from Your hand with love.

Judaism's insistence upon confronting death realistically and directly is also reflected in the requirement that the tearing of a mourner's garment (nowadays often a symbolic ribbon) as a sign of the tear in our hearts must be done while the mourner is standing.

Finally, unlike in many other religions when the mourner leaves the burial site at the cemetery before the casket is lowered into the ground, the Jewish custom at the cemetery after the casket is lowered into the ground in the presence of the mourner is to have the mourners (and others present) bury the deceased by shovelling earth into the grave. As difficult a task as this might be, it emphasizes the reality of death and is literally the last physical act that family and friends can perform the deceased, and helps start the mourner on his or her way to acceptance and reconciliation. The sound of dirt landing on the casket can be a very sobering reminder of death's reality.

SIMPLICITY

The simplicity of the Jewish burial is designed to avert another psychological pitfall. The religious prescription of a wooden casket is meant to avoid ostentation at the funeral, and the simple traditional white linen garment worn by the deceased symbolizes the democracy of death—there is no distinction between the rich and poor, and all are equal in the eyes of God.

COMMUNITY

Especially at a time when a mourner mourns the death of a loved one, one needs the comforting help that other people have to offer. Jewish tradition advocates that the entire Jewish community reach out to the bereaved in the time of their grief and let them know that they are not alone. As an act of kindness, the mourner's first meal after the burial is prepared by others. This is the first opportunity that friends and neighbors have to reach out and comfort the mourners, letting them know that even though they are sad, they are not alone. Traditionally, the congregation moves to the mourner's home and in many communities prayer services are held there during the initial days of mourning.

The Jewish way of life finds order and meaning through structure. Instead of letting death consume mourners, Judaism transforms bereavement into a vehicle with the potential to strengthen family ties, revitalize communal solidarity and promote the sanctity of life itself. Judaism offers consolation in the face of death by reaffirming life, moving mourners slowly back to the normal routine of life.

T W O

BEFORE DEATH

Visiting the sick is a deed of kindness.
—(Talmud Baba Metzia 30)

BIKKUR CHOLIM: VISITING THE SICK

There are several religious obligations that Judaism requires for the living and the dying before death occurs. One of them is *bikkur cholim*, the mitzvah of visiting the sick, one of the supreme acts of holiness.

The rabbis have designated visiting the sick as one of several acts of loving kindness—basic communal obligations of Judaism. A daily prayer states:

> These are the things of which a person enjoys the fruits in this world, while the principal remains in the hereafter, namely: honoring father and mother, practice of kindness, hospitality to strangers, visiting the sick, dowering the bride, attending the dead to the grave.... [based on Mishnah Peah I]

5

From this text we learn that the act of visiting the sick is so very important that it is numbered among those things for which a person enjoys the fruits in this world, while the principal reward is held for him in the world to come.

It is said that God paid Abraham a visit during his recovery after circumcision. The Talmudic rabbis found reference to this visit in Genesis 18:1, where it states that God appeared to Abraham soon after his circumcision. In some communities, including modern day ones, there are special visiting of the sick groups whose task it is to visit those who are confined to hospitals or homes because of illness.

When one visits a sick person, one can bring both physical and psychological relief, calming and lifting the spirit and engendering a feeling of care, warmth, and love.

According to the Talmud, (Nedarim 39b), Rabbi Akiva visited a disciple who became ill and whom no one else would visit. Akiva entered the man's house and "swept and sprinkled the ground before him." When the man recovered, he acknowledged that Akiva had revived him. Akiva immediately lectured his disciples, saying, "One who does not visit the sick is like a shedder of blood." In other words, one's visits to a sick person can make such a significant difference to recovery that to refrain from this obligation is to prolong illness.

In performing the mitzvah of visiting the sick, one can foster the Jewish reverence for life. Akiva's statement underscores the contemporary relevance of ancient and medieval rabbinic teaching about the importance of "bikkur cholim."

In the following Talmudic story, another sage, Rabbi Yochanan, said to his friend Rabbi Elazar, who was seriously ill, "Give me your hand." Rabbi Elazar gave Rabbi Yochanan his hand, and Rabbi Yochanan raised him (Talmud Nedarim 40a). The rabbis teach that a sick person cannot heal himself but needs the help of others. Therefore, one who performs "bikkur cholim" helps to heal a sick person.

Those who visit a sick person are considered blessed because they remove a sixtieth part of the sickness (Talmud Berachot 5b). The importance of each individual in healing an afflicted person cannot be overestimated. The rabbis emphasize, however, that while each visitor removes a sixtieth part of the remaining illness, the illness could never reach zero unless the sick person participates in his or her own healing.

Jewish tradition teaches that it is important to allow others to help us when we are sick. According to a rabbinic tradition, Rabbi Yochanan visited Rabbi Chanina during the latter's illness. When Rabbi Chanina complained about his suffering, Rabbi Yochanan suggested that he speak the same encouraging words to himself that he had spoken with such good effect to Rabbi Yochanan when he was ill. Rabbi Chanina replied, "When I was free of sufferings, I could help others; but now that I am myself a sufferer, I must ask others to help me" (Song of Songs Rabbah 11:16). The meaning of this story is quite obvious: one should know both how to give and how to take, and that in taking, one is also giving.

There are a series of rabbinic guidelines for the practice of "bikkur cholim." For example, it is important that one's visits be made at appropriate times and not last too long, so that one does not make the patient uncomfortable. Jewish law encourages relative and close friends to visit as soon as a person becomes ill. Others should visit after the first three days of illness. (Jerusalem Talmud, Peah 3:7). Because Jewish law prohibits behavior that would endanger one's own life, one is not encouraged to visit where direct contact could cause the visitor to become seriously ill.

Jewish tradition also forbids visiting a person with a severe headache, because visiting might cause an intense strain. This restriction applies by analogy to any visit during which conversation of itself would be injurious to health.

The Code of Jewish Law forbids visits to persons with eye and bowel diseases. These illnesses were considered diseases which cause embarrassment to the afflicted person. Today the listing of embarrassing conditions varies among cultures, age groups and even economic classes. The tradition, however, reflects a general sensitivity to the fact that if the patient would be embarrassed on account of the illness, it is advisable not to visit.

Finally, tradition stresses the view that everyone should visit the sick. Even a prominent person should visit a humble one, the old should visit the young and vice versa, the rich the poor and vice verse. Also, both men and women should visit, and it is a mitzvah to visit non-Jews as well.

Indeed, for people who make it a common practice of visiting the ill, it is said that the benefit flows not only to the person who is ill, but even more so to the visitor.

VIDUI: THE CONFESSION

Rabbi Eliezer once said: "Repent one day before your death." His students asked him, "How are we supposed to know when we will die?" "All the more reason to repent today," he replied, "lest you die tomorrow; and if you repent each day, your whole life will be spent in repentance" (Talmud Shabbat 153a).

Judaism believes in the importance of putting one's house in order, especially when death is on the horizon. In such cases, Judaism has provided a confessional prayer ("vidui") in which a person is able to confess his or her sins before God, for such a time calls for sincere penitence and evokes God's forgiveness.

8

The following is a suggested version of the "viddui." Of course, Jewish tradition allows one to always add one's own personal thoughts, feelings, and prayers.

I acknowledge before you, Adonai my God, and God of my ancestors, that both my cure and my death are in Your hands. May it be Your will to send me perfect healing. Yet if this is not your determination, I will accept it. In Your presence I atone for all my sins and transgressions. O God, bestow upon me the abounding happiness that is treasured up for righteous people. Make known to me the path of life. In Your Presence is fullness of joy. At Your right hand is eternal bliss. Protect my family with whose soul my own is knit. Into Your hand I offer my spirit. You have redeemed me, O God of truth. Amen.

ETHICAL WILLS

Our sages relate that when Jacob, the third biblical patriarch, felt that his end was near he asked for divine mercy: "May it please You to grant that a person should fall ill for two or three days and then be gathered into our people, in order that he may have time to put his house in order and repent of his sins." The Holy One replied: "It shall be so; and you shall be the first to profit by this opportunity" (Zohar, Termuah 174b).

Jacob's blessing to his children (Genesis 49) and the famous farewell address of Moses (Deuteronomy 33) established a most beautiful custom that attained great popularity during the Middle Ages. Parents and grandparents, before their deaths, often wrote letters to their children in which they expressed their hopes and desires for the future, articulating the values they held dear, hoping these principles would live on through their children. Such wills did not deal with the conveyance of things (land, property, jewelry, and the like) to one's heirs. Rather, Jews would take measure of their lives and sum up the truths and values that they wished to transmit to family members. These letters and writings to the children are called ethical wills. The Rabbis regarded such final instructions as of paramount importance and they considered the oral testament of a dying person as legally binding as if his instructions had been written down and witnessed.

Writing an ethical will requires preparation and serious thinking. It will make you probe the essence of your life, the values which you cherish and those which you wish to transmit to members of your family. In writing an ethical will, you will provide your family with a spiritual heritage for which they will be forever grateful. In an ethical will you might express thanks to your spouse, children, or other relatives for their contributions to your life, or you might list values which are part of Judaism's precious heritage and urge that they be carried out.

Following is an ethical will written by Elimelech of Lisensk, and eighteenth century rabbi and founder of the hasidic movement in Galicia.

> One must accustom himself never to initiate conversation with anyone for other than what is urgently required. Even then, one should speak but few words, carefully sifted and screened, so that there be no trace of untruth in his speech, God forbid, nor offense, gossip, slander, insult, nor any manner of ostentation. And one should train himself according to the rule of the sages, "Teach your tongue to say 'I do not know'" (Talmud Berachot 4b; Derech Eretz Zuta, chapter 3).
>
> When engaged in conversation with individuals who are not careful about idle talk, let him evade them with all his might and by any stratagem; and when it is impossible to extricate himself by any means, let him at least keep to a minimum what it is that he must answer them.

One must guard against disliking any fellow Jew except the wicked who are definitely known to him to be beyond judgment in the scale of merit. But if it is possible to judge them in the scale of merit [i.e. by reason of benefit of the doubt] then one is duty bound to love them with all his might, as himself, fulfilling the admonition "love thy neighbor as thyself..."

Above all: Let one guard against intoxicating drink, for this is a vile disease that can lead to extreme degradation. In the words of the Talmudic sage, "... do not imbibe and you will not sin."

Also, one should guard against conversing at all in the synagogue, even words of moral instruction, lest he be led thereby to indulge in idle speech.

THREE

FROM DEATH TO BEREAVEMENT

Praised are You, God, who is the true Judge.
—(Kriah Blessing)

ANINUT: EXEMPTION FROM RELIGIOUS DUTIES

When death finally occurs, even if such a death is expected or anticipated, news of it can throw one into a state of shock, panic, and confusion. In Jewish practice, the first phase of the Jewish mourning process is called "aninut." The person who has experienced the death of a relative is called an "onen." Aninut begins when one learns of the death and ends with burial. During this emotionally laden period, many decisions may be required, but mourners may not always be ready to make them. Because of the need to make and conclude the funeral arrangements, Jewish law (using wise psychology), releases the onen from the obligations of prayer, social amenities, and other kinds of mitzvot. The laws which govern the actions of an onen are sensitive to his or her inner struggle, and reflect a common sense understanding of a mourner's current state of mind. Traditional Jewish law states that an onen should not drink wine, eat meat, or say a blessing before or after eating, nor should he or she indulge in luxuries or pleasures, or conduct business and professional activities. On the Sabbath or on a festival, an onen is permitted to follow the appropriate public observances of the day, which include eating meat, drinking wine and reciting blessings.

Most friends refrain from visiting the home of the bereaved until after the burial, allowing the family private time. Close friends, however, often assist with the funeral arrangements.

Children at this time may see adults in a state of confusion and disorientation, anger and bewilderment. Sometimes the sorrow is extremely deep, seemingly endless. This is quite normal. It is important for children to know that the community of friends usually reach out to the bereaved family in their time of grief to let them know that they are not alone. The rabbi too, will likely visit the home and offer his or her comfort and spiritual support.

Aninut, Judaism's first stage of mourning is designed to help the newly bereaved acknowledge and accept one's pain and loss.

WHO IS A MOURNER?

According to Jewish law, one is obliged to mourn for a father, mother, son, daughter, brother, sister (including a half-brother and a half-sister), husband, or wife. The biblical source for this law is Leviticus 21:1–3: "And God spoke to Moses saying, 'Speak to the priests, the sons of Aaron, and say to them that none of them shall defile himself for the dead among his people, except for his nearest of kin: his mother, father, son, daughter, brother, or sister.'" Later tradition made explicit the requirement to mourn for one's spouse.

Males from the age of thirteen years and one day and females from the age of twelve years and one day may observe the laws of mourning. Children under this age, while not considered mourners, may engage in some of the mourning customs and traditions if they choose to do so. Judaism also does not limit the observance of mourning rites to only these relatives. One may mourn for whomever one chooses.

WHEN DEATH OCCURS

As soon as one learns of the death of a loved one, one should call one's rabbi, who in turn will notify the "hevra kaddisha," the burial society, if there is one in your community. Next, a call will need to be placed to the funeral home to make arrangements for the transfer of the deceased, the funeral, and the burial. This includes setting the date and time of the funeral.

Preserving the dignity of life and of the human body sets the tone for the Jewish response to death. Historically, every family had the responsibility to care for its own dead. Today, this task has been assumed by a group of caring men and women called the "hevra kaddisha," meaning "holy society." In some modern synagogues the hevra kaddisha is called the caring committee. This group of people (who are among the first to be informed of a death in the community) are familiar with Jewish funerary practices and help the mourners prepare their loved one for burial.

Just as a baby is washed and enters the world clean and pure, so does a Jewish person leave the world cleansed by the religious act of "tahara," purification. Caring for the body from the time of death until burial is considered an act of real kindness. In Hebrew this act of kindness is called "kevod hamet"—honor to the deceased. The biblical commentator Rashi once noted, in commenting on chapter 47, verse 29 of Genesis (when Jacob as an old man asks his son Joseph to arrange for his burial in the Land of Israel), that caring for the dead is the truest act of kindness, since one does it without any expectation of repayment. The body of the dead is clothed in plain white linen, cotton, or muslin shroud, "tachrichim" in Hebrew. The Talmud records that at one time the bodies of the wealthy were brought to burial on a richly ornamented stately bed, while the bodies of the poor were brought to burial on a plain platform (Moed Katan 27a,b). This practice brought embarrassment to the poor, resulting in a law that was instituted that required all of the dead—rich and poor alike, to be brought to burial on a plain platform. The dead at that time were not buried in coffins, just as they are not buried in coffins in contemporary Israel.

The Talmud also records that at one time the expense of burying the dead was harder to bear than the fact of death itself. It reached the point of some families choosing to abandon the bodies of relatives to escape the burden of expense. Then the renowned Rabban Gamaliel left instructions that he be buried in plain linen shrouds rather than in expensive garments which he and his family could easily have afforded. His act set an impressive precedent, and since that time Jewish tradition has insisted on simple burial with a minimum of expense. Today the plain white linen shroud symbolizes the democracy of death, that all people are equal in the eyes of God.

A deceased male (and a female who elects to do so) is also customarily draped in a prayer shawl ("tallit") with one "tzitzit" (fringe) cut off, making it unfit for further use. The hevra kaddisha also sprinkles a small bag of soil from Israel into the coffin. In this way the loved one will always be touching earth from the land of the Jewish people.

According to Jewish tradition, a dead body is not to be left alone before the funeral. Although some sources trace this practice to the necessity of protecting the body from harm, not leaving the body unattended is essentially another way of showing respect to the dead. In traditional settings, a person called a "shomer" (literally, watchperson) will stay with the deceased from the time of death until burial. A candle is placed near the deceased and the shomer often reads Psalm (especially Psalm 23 and 91).

Originally it was customary for each cemetery to have a tahara room for the purpose of the rite of purification. Today, since so many funerals take place in funeral homes, the rite of purification is done on their premises.

Jewish tradition frowns upon the viewing of the body. Although it has become the widespread American custom (in non-Jewish settings) to have the body on exhibition the night before the funeral, the practice is contrary to Jewish tradition. The dead are not to be put on display. It is improper to apply cosmetics to the dead, and the coffin, once closed after the preparation by the hevra kaddisha, it is not be opened again. Thus Judaism encourages one to remember one's loved ones in the vibrancy of their lives.

In Reform, Reconstructionist and other more liberal settings, personal autonomy with regard to burial may allow the deceased to be buried in clothing other than white linen shrouds. Other deviations from Jewish prescription may also occur as well.

CASKETS

Although some mourners are tempted to purchase caskets which they think will last forever, our tradition takes its advice from the text in Genesis 3:19: "Dust you are and to the dust you shall return." Thus Jewish law requires that the casket be made entirely of wood, allowing it, when buried, to return naturally to the earth. Although the selection of a casket is a personal one, often determined by local custom, simple unostentatious caskets have always been preferred in Jewish tradition. In Israel, where wood is scarce, no casket is used at all. Rather, the deceased is buried in a wrapped shroud.

THE FUNERAL

Historically, Jewish funerals took place at the home of the deceased or at the cemetery. Synagogues were used very rarely, and only for people of extraordinary distinction and stature in the community.

Today, some communities permit funerals (for rabbis and leaders of the congregation, such as the president) to be held in the synagogue. In this way, the entire celebration and sanctification of life throughout the life cycle is associated with the synagogue. Death is not segregated in an institution of its own but becomes a part of daily living.

On the other hand, funeral homes are designed to make sure that everything runs smoothly. If neither a Jewish funeral home or a synagogue is available for the funeral, then a Gentile funeral home is permissible.

The Hebrew word for funeral—"levayah"—means "accompanying," teaching that the nature of a Jewish funeral implies involvement. It is a mitzvah and an act of respect not only to attend the funeral service, but especially to actually accompany the dead, walking behind the coffin for at least a few feet immediately after the funeral or at the cemetery.

Usually the mourners arrive at the funeral before family, friends and relatives. Some funeral chapels have a "family room" into which the mourners are directed upon their arrival. As other people arrive, they may be directed (at the request of the mourners) to the room in which the mourners are seated. There they may offer their personal condolences. At other times, mourners may decide that they need their time of privacy and opt not to greet family and friends before the funeral.

Before the funeral service begins, all but the mourners are directed to the room where the service will take place. A ceremony known as "kriah," the rending of the garments, is often performed at this time. There are other customs of "kriah" that call for doing it at the moment of hearing of the death, wherever the mourner may be at the time, or at the cemetery, prior to the burial. A tear is made on the mourner's clothing (or on a symbolic black ribbon attached to the clothing in more nontraditional settings) as an outward sign of grief and mourning and as an acceptance of death. This custom originated with our biblical ancestors Jacob, David and Job, who cut their clothing after experiencing the death of a loved one. The ceremony of kriah provides the mourners with an opportunity for psychological relief, allowing the mourner to express anguish and anger through an act of destruction made sacred by Jewish tradition.

For the loss of a parent, the cutting is customarily on the left side, closest to the heart. For all others, kriah is customarily on the right side. Immediately prior to the cutting, the mourner recites the following benediction: "Baruch ata Adonai Elohenu Melech ha'olam dayan ha-emet. Praised are You, Adonai our God, Sovereign of the Universe, the true Judge." The benediction is intended as a reaffirmation of our faith in God and in the worthwhileness of life, even during a time of great sorrow. This custom also recognizes God as the final Judge of all people.

Contrary to popular belief, there is no standard or fixed funeral service. Generally the rabbi will read a selection from the Book of Psalms, then deliver a eulogy in which the attributes of the deceased are remembered. It is considered an honor and an important obligation for mourners and family members to provide insights for the eulogy. Abraham, the first patriarch, eulogized his own wife Sarah. Today at many funerals family members are encouraged to speak words of tribute to their loved one. "Eil Malei Rahamim", a prayer to God that the soul may find eternal rest, generally concludes the funeral service.

The recessional, performed by wheeling the casket from the funeral chapel or synagogue to the hearse, is often attended to by honorary pallbearers chosen by the family. This is another way of demonstrating honor to the deceased. The Talmud illustrates the importance of this mitzvah when it says (Ketubot 17a): "One must abandon the study of Torah to carry the dead to their resting place." The practice of friends and family carrying their loved ones to the grave dates back to biblical times, when Jacob's sons carried him into the land of Canaan and buried him there. (Genesis 50:13) The rabbi often will lead the recessional while reciting psalms.

Many parents wonder and worry about whether their younger children should attend the funeral services of someone they loved. Are the children too young and will it be too traumatic? There really are no set answers, but experience has shown that even a young child can benefit significantly from sharing in some of the rituals that attend death, provided that he or she has been properly prepared to know what to expect and to be open with questions. Parents are often the best judges of whether and how their children should participate in a funeral. Rabbi Earl Grollman, a leading expert in explaining death to children, believes that if a child is old enough to attend a synagogue and comprehend in part what is taking place, that child ought to be allowed to attend a funeral to say farewell to a significant person in his or her life.

If the funeral is taking place in a funeral chapel rather than in a familiar synagogue, it would be sensible to explain in advance to younger children what the chapel looks like, where they will be sitting, and other details. It is important to let children know that some people may be crying at the funeral, and that tears are not evidence of weakness, but rather a way of expressing the pain of separation. When Sarah the matriarch died, her husband Abraham "came to mourn and to weep for her" (Genesis 23:2).

No matter how helpful and therapeutic the funeral may be, children ought not to be forced to attend. Some apprehensive youngsters may elect to remain at home, and ought not to be "shamed" into going.

Many times the question arises as to the permissibility of flowers at a Jewish funeral. Although the Talmud mentioned the use of flowers centuries ago, the current practice is to discourage their use, following the principle of keeping funerals simple, as well as resisting the introduction of alien customs. Although Sephardic custom does allow for flowers, well-wishers ought to be encouraged to give "tzedakah" (charity) as a more lasting memorial.

ATTENDING THE FUNERAL OF A NON-JEWISH FRIEND OR RELATIVE

Among the Orthodox, attendance at a non-Jewish funeral is generally not permitted, especially if the ceremony takes place in the church itself. The other branches of Judaism would be more likely to permit and even encourage their members to attend the funeral of a non-Jew.

Non-Jewish funerals have some elements with which you may wish to become accustomed. For instance, the wake is fairly common in non-Jewish settings. It provides an occasion for neighbors and relatives to visit the bereaved family and pay their respects. Most wakes today take place in a funeral chapel, with specific hours designated for visiting.

The funeral director will usually arrange the casket for visitors to pay their respects and provide chairs for the family to receive visitors. Visitors generally go directly to the family, offer a brief word of sympathy and then proceed to the casket to say a prayer. If the casket is open, the body is usually dressed in fine clothing and can look quite life-like.

The Roman Catholic funeral is a prayer service that is usually incorporated into the celebration of Mass. It is usually held a few days after the death to allow for the wake. It commences at the funeral home with a procession to the church. The casket is covered with a white pall, symbolic of the white robe of baptism. The priest wears white vestments to express the joy of faith that overcomes the sadness of death. A candle, symbolic of Jesus, is placed at the casket. Various readings and a eulogy typically follow, including musical presentations, often chosen by members of the deceased's family.

In Protestant ritual, the church sanctuary is often the place for the funeral, but it can be held in either the home or a funeral chapel. The service itself is conducted by the minister, according to local church tradition. Although the ritual varies, it will generally consist of a reading from the Bible, prayer offerings, and a funeral sermon or meditation which focuses on the mourning process of the bereaved. Sometimes there is a formal eulogy, although many Protestant clergy today do not include one. Funeral music, played on the organ, is an important part of the service, and is usually accompanied by congregational singing. When there is an open casket, it is customary for people who so choose to file by it at the end of the funeral service.

At the cemetery the official rite for both Protestants and Catholics is quite brief. There is a blessing of the grave, a biblical reading and several prayers. As a rule, the bereaved family does not remain at the cemetery for the burial, although there appears to be a growing trend for them to remain, as is done in Judaism.

The custom of having friends return to the family's home after the burial for a small collation varies from one local to another. While there is no "shiva," some Christians go to a restaurant or return home to greet friends.

There are several ways in which one may appropriately express his or her sorrow to a non-Jewish person. These would include: a sympathy card or condolence letter to the family, a phone call to the family, a visit to the funeral parlor and attendance at the wake, a memorial gift to a charity in memory of the deceased, and undertaking a specific act on behalf of the bereaved (e.g. bringing food).

AT THE CEMETERY : THE BURIAL

Arriving at the cemetery, pallbearers from among the family and friends customarily carry the casket to the grave. Again this custom harks back to Jacob's children carrying him to his grave. In traditional burials, seven stops are customarily made by the pallbearers on their way to the grave, recalling the seven times the word "vanity" appears in the Book of Ecclesiastes. Between the stops, the comforting Psalm 91 is recited.

A prayer called "Tzidduk HaDin", which is an acceptance of God's judgment, is usually recited at the graveside. Its words begin: "The Rock, God's work is perfect, for all God's ways are judgment. A God of faithfulness and without sin, just and right is God." This prayer is intended as an affirmation of life, especially at a time when the mourners may feel like rejecting the value of life itself or their faith in God.

The rabbi or family members may then say a few closing words, followed by the lowering of the casket into the grave. This is followed by the Eil Malei Rahamim, the prayer for the peace of the departed soul, and the mourner's Kaddish. The Kaddish is a most hallowed prayer, sanctified by its association with death, although there is nothing specifically about death in it. It is an affirmation of life, proclaiming the eternity of God, God's mercy and sovereignty.

It is considered a mitzvah, a religious duty, for relatives and friends to help shovel the earth back into the grave to cover the casket. As difficult as it may seem, this is literally the last physical act that family and friends can perform for the deceased, and helps start the mourner on his or her way to acceptance and reconciliation. The sound of dirt landing on the coffin can be a very sobering reminder of death's reality. There is a custom of not passing the shovel directly from one person to another, but rather placing the shovel on the ground before the next person picks it up. This gesture symbolizes the hope that the tragedy of death will not pass from one person to another. In a less traditional setting, the coffin is covered with a carpet simulating grass and is not lowered until the mourners leave.

Other private rituals have developed over the years and vary from place to place. For instance, some Jews pull up a few blades of grass as they leave the cemetery, symbolizing faith in an afterlife. Just as the plucked grass grows again, so we and our loved ones vow to go on living.

Others wash their hands upon leaving the cemetery as a rite of purification after being in contact with the deceased. This is generally performed upon entering the house of mourning to begin the period of shiva.

With the burying of the deceased, the emphasis shifts from honoring the deceased to comforting the mourners. To act out this transition, all of those present are often asked by the officiant to form two parallel lines, facing each other. As the mourners pass through the two lines, those present recite the following traditional words of comfort: "HaMakom yenachem etkhem betokh sha'ar avlai Zion v'Yerushalayim." "May God comfort you now among the mourners for Zion and Jerusalem."

SEPHARDIC BURIAL CUSTOMS

Jews of Sephardic origin follow most of the traditional aforementioned burial customs. There are some differences, though, from Ashenazic custom. Among Syrian Jews, for example, surviving children ask forgiveness from the deceased parent. A shofar (ram's horn) is sounded at the funeral of a man with children before the recitation of the mourner's Kaddish. Traditionally, women weep and cry openly at the news of death. In some Syrian communities, men and women are buried in separate sections of the cemetery. Finally, *kriah*, the rending of the garment, is often performed when the mourners return home, and not at the cemetery.

FOUR

MOURNING OBSERVANCES

Silence is meritorious in a house of mourning.
—(Talmud Berachot 6b)

PAYING A SHIVA VISIT

Immediately after the burial the family of the bereaved returns to their home to "sit" shiva. Shiva, taken from the Hebrew word for "seven," refers to the first seven days of mourning. Since Jewish tradition reckons parts of a day to be considered as a whole day, the day of the interment is considered the first day of mourning regardless of whether it included a full twenty-four hours or not.

Shiva officially begins after the deceased has been interred and traditionally lasts for seven days. When first arriving at home from the funeral, the mourners eat a meal called "seudat havra'a" (meal of consolation). This is the first opportunity that friends and neighbors have to reach out and comfort the mourners, letting them know that even though they are overcome by grief, they are not alone. Usually, this meal consists of round foods, especially eggs. Round foods are a reminder of the cycle of life, which inevitably includes death. Eggs, in particular, symbolize new life which goes on, even in the face of death.

In Judaism, there is always a creative tension between personal or community joy and sorrow. This pull is felt at various times and seasons during the year when a death occurs. Thus, when a death occurs on the first day of a major festival (Passover, Shavuot, Sukkot), the beginning of shiva is delayed until the end of the festival. Moreover, onset of a major festival brings the shiva period to an end regardless of how many days have elapsed. A wedding celebration may also change the laws for mourning, and it is best to check with your rabbi when a question of observance arises.

Shiva is divided into two parts. The first three days following the burial are a period of intense grief. Thus, some Reform and Reconstructionist rabbis have abbreviated shiva to this period only. During this period, in recognition of the overwhelming nature of one's loss, Jewish tradition encourages the mourner to stay at home. Friends are encouraged to visit after the mourner has had a chance to deal privately with his or her grief.

Following this beginning, the mourner enters the next and final stage in the remainder of the shiva. Friends and relatives are likely to come and try to do their best to comfort the mourner and provide for his or her daily needs.

The day of the burial counts as the first day of shiva, and shiva ends on the morning of the seventh day. Shabbat, the Sabbath, is included in counting the seven days, though on Shabbat no outward signs of mourning apply (i.e. mourners are allowed to wear regular shoes, sit on regular chairs and attend synagogue services).

On Friday (unless it is the seventh day of shiva), on the day before a festival, shiva is observed until two and one-half hours before sunset. On Passover eve it ends at noon. A festival, Rosh Hashanah or Yom Kippur, *annuls the remainder* of shiva, provided that the mourner has first observed at least one hour of shiva.

WHAT ONE MAY SEE IN A HOUSE OF MOURNING

Certain shiva practices are done immediately upon returning from the cemetery. First, traditionally, one washes the hands. It is an ancient custom to cleanse when leaving the presence of death and to rid oneself of spiritual impurities associated with it. During the shiva itself, mourners traditionally sit lower than others, usually on low stools and do not wear leather shoes. Both practices are signs of mourning, indicating a significant change from the typical patterns of normative daily life and physically reflect the emotional state of bereavement.

A shiva candle, which burns throughout the seven day period of mourning, is customarily lit by the bereaved upon entering the house of shiva after the funeral service. In Proverbs 20:27 a person's soul is likened to light, and the candle thus reminds all who visit of the gathering's purpose. Mirrors in a house of shiva are customarily covered. In this way the mourners are able to focus on their relationship with the deceased and not on personal vanity.

During the period of shiva, a traditional mourner customarily abstains from business and professional activities, sexual intercourse, bathing or anointing the body, using cosmetics and cutting hair. If severe financial loss would result from not working, the mourner is permitted to return to work after observing the mourning for three days, including a brief observance the third day.

Very often a minyan (an assembly of ten persons) will assemble in the house of shiva, allowing the mourner to say the mourner's

Kaddish, either in the morning, or the evening, or both morning and evening.

Among most Sephardic communities, the traditional meal of condolence at a house of shiva is prepared by the hevra kaddisha or family and friends. Mourners sit on the floor on pillows, not on low stools. Daily services are held in the home and the Zohar, the Book of Mysticism, is studied throughout the week.

COMFORTING MOURNERS

It is an important religious duty to visit mourners, especially during the week after the death of their relatives. This custom of offering consolation to the bereaved is very ancient. The Bible refers to it several times. In the Book of Job, however, we have the most vivid description of friends visiting the unfortunate Job in his hour of sadness: "They sat down upon the ground with him seven days and seven nights."

During shiva the custom is for friends and members of the community to come and formally express their condolences. Many people are uncomfortable in a house of shiva, and are not exactly sure of what to say, searching for just the right words. In fact, they may be inclined not to speak until spoken to, and this in fact is what Jewish tradition instructs. Visitors are there to support the mourner, even in silence. A warm embrace or an arm around the shoulders are wonderful nonverbal messages to the bereaved.

Visitors who do converse with the mourners should remember that they are not expected to cheer them up in their time of anguish. One does not console by attempting to distract the mourner. A person finds greatest comfort in talking about his or her dear ones who have passed on, by recalling meaningful incidents in their lives that were not known or may have been forgotten by the family. When speaking of the deceased and reminiscing, a Hebrew phrase is generally added: "alav hashalom" (may he rest in peace) or "aleha hashalom" (may she rest in peace). "Zikhrono livrakha" (for a male) and "zikhronah livrakhah" (for a female) are also used, meaning "of blessed memory."

The traditional condolence statement to the mourner is: "HaMakom yenachem etkhem b'tokh sha'ar avelei Zion v'Yerushalayim. May God comfort you among the mourners for Zion and Jerusalem."

When visiting a house of shiva is not possible, a phone call or condolence letter is also greatly appreciated by the bereaved. When writing a letter one should express one's inner feelings by using words of sympathy that express one's sorrow. It is wise to avoid cliches and truisms and speak from the heart. Noting one's personal memories of the deceased, reflecting the impact that he or she had on one's life, and mentioning any outstanding qualities are cherished by the bereaved. Finally, reminding the mourner that he is not alone in his grief and concluding the letter with some words of love can be extremely comforting.

THE CONCLUSION OF SHIVA

Shiva concludes on the morning of the seventh day. When mourners get up from shiva, they walk a short distance, usually around the block in their neighborhood, to symbolize their return to society and the real world, from which death forced them to withdraw. Although there are no prescribed prayers that need to be said, many modern day meditations and readings have been created for recitation of the mourner upon concluding the shiva. Following are two suggested readings for concluding shiva:

O God, Healer of shattered hearts, let neither death nor sorrow have dominion over us. May we always remember and cherish all of those good and kind deeds in the life of _____. May his/her memory inspire us to deeds of loving-kindness.

We rise up now to face life's tasks once more. There will always be moments of loneliness, for a loved one has passed from our midst. Teach us to always be thankful for the life of our dear companion and for the opportunity of sharing so many joyous moments with him/her. May we always honor _____ by rising above despair and finding consolation in serving our people. Amen.

FIVE

Post-Mourning Practices

When a person sheds tears at the death of a virtuous person, the Holy One counts them and places them in His treasure house.

—(Talmud Shabbat 105a)

SHLOSHIM

Shloshim ("thirty") refers to the first thirty days following the death of a loved one. The period from the end of shiva to the end of shloshim is one of transition from deep bereavement to resuming life's normal routine. During this period a mourner customarily does not wear new clothes or cut one's hair, or participate in general festivities, and avoids public places of entertainment. A mourner also does not attend parties celebrating a "brit milah" (circumcision), a "pidyon haben" (redemption of the first born), or a wedding, though he or she is permitted to attend the ceremonies. When mourning a parent's death, restrictions continue until twelve months after the day of death. Jewish festivals affect the length and determination of shloshim. For example, if mourning has been observed for at least one hour before a festival, shiva is ended by that festival. In that event, shloshim ends fifteen days after the last day of Passover or Shavuot, and eight days after the last day of Sukkot. When shiva is completed before a festival, shloshim ends when the festival begins. When shiva is completed before Rosh Hashanah, shloshim ends when Yom Kippur begins, and when shiva ends before Yom Kippur, shloshim ends with Sukkot. One should always consult with one's rabbi whenever a question of observance arises.

MOURNER'S KADDISH

A mourner first recites the Kaddish at the cemetery after burial. This particular Kaddish is known as the burial Kaddish, because it includes a paragraph about the eventual resurrection of the dead, during the messianic era. Many rabbis also use the regular mourner's Kaddish at graveside.

The Kaddish prayer originally referred to a brief prayer and response recited at the close of rabbinic lessons in the ancient house of study. Such lessons would end with a discourse containing a message of consolation. The Kaddish extended that message as a prayer of messianic hope. The actual name of God is not mentioned in the Kaddish, which emphasizes hallowing and praising God through redemption of life in this world and through the universal acceptance of God's sovereignty.

The word "Kaddish" itself is an Aramaic word meaning holy. Recitation of the Kaddish is an act of hallowing and praising God's name. In Jewish tradition, such an act must take place in public assembly, which is defined as at least a quorum of ten adults (minyan).

The expression "you are my kaddishel" among Ashkenazi Jews

means "you are the one who will say Kaddish for me after I am gone." Traditionally, a son is required to say the Kaddish for his deceased parents. Reform, Conservative, and Reconstructionist branches of Judaism have understood this obligation as binding on the daughter as well. These responsibilities cannot be transferred to another person. However, one may want to say Kaddish for someone other than a parent. In the past, traditional families often paid individuals to say Kaddish for their deceased, particularly when their was no male survivor to say it. Such a practice is discouraged in liberal Jewish settings.

In many Reform synagogues all congregants are encouraged to rise in unison and recite the Kaddish. This custom expresses solidarity with the bereaved, and also allows for the recitation of the Kaddish for those who may not have anyone to do so (e.g. those who perished in the Holocaust leaving no survivors).

At the end of shloshim it is appropriate for family and friends to gather together to read or study appropriate texts and to speak about the deceased.

The recitation of the mourner's Kaddish is for eleven months. The mourner's Kaddish is also traditionally recited on each anniversary of the death (yahrzeit), and at Yizkor Memorial services on Yom Kippur, Sukkot, Passover, and Shavuot.

THE TOMBSTONE AND MARKER

Like many Jewish customs, the custom of erecting a monument over a grave dates back to biblical times. The Book of Genesis 35:20 describes Jacob when he set a pillar upon his wife Rachel's grave. He undoubtedly did this to keep his wife's memory alive as well as to be able to identify the grave.

There are several customs regarding inscriptions on the tombstone itself. The English name of the deceased, the Hebrew name, and both the secular and Hebrew date of death often appear on the tombstone. Sometimes above the name of the deceased, especially among the Ashkenazim, one finds two Hebrew letters, פ נ, which are the letters for פה נח ("po nach"—here rests). The Sephardim often use the Hebrew letters מ ק standing for קבורה מצבת ("matzevet kevurah"), meaning "monument of the grave of." Underneath the inscription one usually finds the Hebrew letters תנצב״ה standing for תהי נשמתו צרורה בצרור החיים (*tehi nishmato tzerurah bitzeror hachayyim*) "May his soul be bound up in the bond of eternal life."

A Levites tombstone often has an ewer carved out over the inscriptions as a symbol of his office, because in the ancient Temple the Levites washed the priest's hands before they delivered the Priestly Blessing.

The tombstones of kohanim, descendants of the ancient priests, are often marked by a carving of the hands raised in the Priestly Benediction.

Occasionally there will be a verse from the Bible or rabbinic literature (or from any Jewish text) on the tombstone. The verse is usually chosen because it has some application to the life of the deceased and the family decides that it will serve as an appropriate memorial.

THE UNVEILING

In Western countries and in America it is customary to consecrate the tombstone with a service. Since in America the custom is to remove a cloth which is draped over the tombstone, the ritual is known as the unveiling.

The unveiling ceremony generally takes place within a year after the death. In actuality, it can take place anytime after thirty days.

The service itself offers another opportunity for the family of the deceased to pay tribute to their loved one and to ponder the meaning of both life and death.

Caution should be taken so that the unveiling does not become a social event or another funeral. It is appropriate for the immediate family and closest relatives and friends to be invited to the ceremony. Although there is often a rabbi to officiate, many clergypersons today are encouraging families to lead their own unveilings, since the ceremony is relatively brief and simple.

Most unveilings consist of the reading of several psalms, a few brief remarks about the deceased, the removal of the cloth covering the monument and the reading of the inscription, the chanting of the Eil Malei Rahamim and the reciting of the mourner's Kaddish if ten persons are present. Reform Judaism allows this even if a minyan of ten is not present.

At the conclusion of the ceremony the custom is to place a small stone or pebble on the tombstone. Laying stones on monuments is a sign that someone visited the cemetery and thus an acknowledgment that the deceased is still loved and remembered.

VISITING THE GRAVE

Judaism has always tried to discourage excessive visitations to the grave. However, there are suggested times that are appropriate for visiting a grave (and these are the times also appropriate for an unveiling). The most appropriate days for grave visitation are the days that concludes the shloshim, the day of the yahrzeit (anniversary of the death), traditional fast days such as Tisha B'Av, and anytime during the month of Elul, especially the day before Rosh Hashanah. Visitation ought not to be made on the Sabbath or Passover, Sukkot, and Shavuot, including the intermediate days.

Whenever one visits the cemetery one is free to recite or read whatever prayer or psalm that one chooses. One popular custom is to use Psalm 119, the verses of which are grouped in alphabetical order. One tradition is to read those verses which begin with the letters of the name of the deceased. The Eil Malei Rahamim and the recitation of the mourner's Kaddish (in the presence of a minyan of ten) are other prayers said when visiting the grave.

YAHRZEIT: ANNIVERSARY OF THE DEATH

Jewish tradition has added a special ritual to help the mourner meet the crisis of bereavement. This is the annual commemoration of the anniversary of death known as "yahrzeit" in Yiddish ("year time") and as "anos" among Sephardic Jews. Each year, on the anniversary of the death, a special day is consecrated to one's loved ones. Traditionally this is done on the anniversary of the death according to the Hebrew calendar, but some people use secular dates to mark the yahrzeit. If one is not certain of the day when a loved one died, one should select an appropriate date to observe yahrzeit each year.

The yahrzeit officially begins with the lighting of a twenty-four hour candle on the night of the anniversary. Light is symbolic of a person's soul, suggesting immortality. "The soul of a person," says the Book of Proverbs (20:27), "is the lamp of God."

When lighting a candle there is no traditional prayer that is recited. Today numerous meditations and prayers have been created for precisely this occasion. Here is a suggested yahrzeit prayer when lighting the candle:

> I now remember my dear _____ who has gone to his/her eternal resting place. May his/her soul be given everlasting life, and may his/her memory be a source of blessing and an inspiration to those who knew and loved him/her.

The light is now kindled and one then says:

Zichrono (Zichrona) livracha—May his (her) memory serve as a blessing.

On the day of the yahrzeit itself, the traditional custom is to attend services and recite the mourner's Kaddish. The Eil Malei Rachamim is chanted by the prayer leader in memory of the deceased. It is entirely proper for the one who has yahrzeit to act as the leader of the service, if capable of doing so. On the Sabbath preceding the yahrzeit it is also customary to call the one who has yahrzeit to the Torah for an aliyah.

Appropriate too is the fulfillment of some mitzvah in honor of the deceased on the day of the yahrzeit. This might consist of Torah study and contributing to some worthy cause. It is also appropriate for family and friends to gather on the yahrzeit for the purpose of recalling various aspects of the life of their loved one, thereby perpetuating his or her memory in a warm and loving family atmosphere.

YIZKOR

The association of memorial services with joyous holy days is very characteristic of Judaism. On Yom Kippur, Shemini Atzeret, Passover, and Shavuot, a remembrance service called Yizkor takes place. Participating in this service allows one to remember their loved ones and the values they cherished and transmitted while alive. In this way they are encouraged to continue to lead the good lives that their loved ones bequeathed to them.

The ancient custom of remembering the dead is referred to in the Apocrypha, where we read that Judah Maccabee "took a collection amounting to two thousand silver drachmas, each person contributing, and sent it to Jerusalem to pray for the dead. He made atonement for the dead, so that they might be set free from their sin" (II Maccabees 12:43-45).

Yizkor may be recited for all Jewish dead: parents, grandparents, husbands and wives, children, family, and friends. Some people do not say Yizkor for friends or grandparents if their parents are living. Despite the common practice, which suggests it, Yizkor may be recited on the very first holy day after death.

The Yizkor service consists of biblical passages related to the meaning of life and death, passages specifically directed are remembering our loved ones (including Jewish Martyrs and those killed in the Holocaust), the Eil Malei Rahamim, in which God is asked to shelter the souls of our beloved in eternal peace, and the mourner's Kaddish. Psalm 23 ("The Lord is my Shepherd") is also often recited in many synagogues today.

As with yahrzeit, it is also customary to kindle a twenty-four hour candle on the evening preceding Yizkor. The custom is also to pledge charity and perform other kind deeds to honor the memory of the departed.

Contrary to popular opinion, a person with a living parent may attend yizkor services.

SIX

SPECIAL SITUATIONS AND CONCERNS

There are a number of issues related to the Jewish way of death and dying that are in need of special exploration and discussion. This chapter will summarize these so-called special cases, many of which deal with issues regarding the sanctity of the body in Jewish law.

SUICIDE

For Judaism, God owns everything, including our bodies. God loans them to people for the duration of their lives, and they are to be returned to God at the time of death. This being the case, only God can give life or take it. Therefore suicide, the taking of one's own life, is morally wrong, traditionally considered an act of blasphemy and a transgression of Jewish law. Although the Bible does not have an explicit prohibition against suicide, the following verse has been interpreted in the Talmud Baba Kama 91b as the prohibition of suicide:

> And surely your blood of your lives will I require; at the hand of every beast will I require it; and at the hand of man, even at the hand of every man's brother, will I require the life of man. (Genesis 9:5)

Rabbi Eleazar is quoted in the Talmud as saying: "I will require your blood if taken by your own hands."

As far as Judaism is concerned, whether a death is a suicide is not solely determined by police records or decisions rendered by the court, but by a rabbi after a careful consideration of all of the variables, which includes the influence of drugs, state of mental well-being, motivation, and planning.

Post-talmudic authorities considered suicide a most heinous transgression, even worse than murder. It was thought to be a denial of the Jewish doctrine of reward and punishment, the world to come, and the sovereignty of God, and the opinion was expressed that the suicide forfeits his portion in the world to come.

Several definite suicides are recorded in the Bible: Samson (Judges 16:30), Saul and his armor-bearer (I Samuel 31:4–5), and Ahithophel (II Samuel 17:23). Of course the most famous act of suicide in Jewish history was the mass suicide of the Jewish zealots atop of Masada.

It was in the last post-talmudic tractate of Semachot (Evel Rabbati 2:1–5) that the laws regarding suicide are formulated. It laid down that no rites are to be performed in honor of the dead (e.g. the rite of kriah and delivering a eulogy), but everything which appertains to respect for the mourners is permitted.

Quite a number of rabbis today feel that the laws regarding suicide are insensitive to the mental anguish suffered by the person who commits suicide, as well as by the survivors. In addition, even traditional Judaism asserts that the customary mourning practices should be observed in every detail, even in a case of a suicide, if not doing so would lead to the family's honor being questioned.

A distinction in Jewish law is made between a suicide while of sound mind—to which the restrictions apply, and suicide while of unsound mind, to which they do not apply. The suicide of a minor is not regarded as culpable. Only where there is the clearest evidence of deliberate intent is a suicide to be considered as being of sound mind.

Jewish people have always been sensitive to the state of mind which would lead any person to commit suicide. Thus, only rarely are self-inflicted deaths labeled as suicides within the context of Jewish law.

CREMATION

While liberal Judaism allows for cremation, it is traditionally prohibited because it does not allow for the body to naturally return to the earth. The passage in Deuteronomy 21:23 "his body shall not remain all night upon the tree, but you shall surely bury him the same day" has been advanced as a scriptural proof text, as well as other biblical sayings such as "for dust you are, and unto dust you shall return" (Genesis 3:19). Cremation, however, was not unknown to the early Israelites, and "burning" was one of the four death penalties imposed by the biblical code for a number of offenses (Leviticus 20:14; 21:9). The ancient rabbis, however, found the execution of this death sentence so abhorrent that they refused to interpret the injunction literally (Talmud Sanhedrin 7:2). In biblical times, cremation was clearly considered to be a humiliation inflicted on criminals (Joshua 7:15), and the practice as such was condemned, even when it involved the burning of the remains of an Edomite King as described in the Book of Amos 2:1.

The Talmud (Avodah Zarah 1:3) considers the burning of a corpse to be an idolatrous practice, and the Talmud Sanhedrin 46b deduced that burial is a positive commandment prescribed in Deuteronomy 21:23.

For the rabbis, cremation was a denial of the belief of bodily resurrection and an affront to the dignity of the human body. Today too, rabbinic opinion often compares cremation to the destruction of Jews in the crematoria of the Holocaust, a horrendous reminder of the evil and savagery that one group of people can perpetuate upon another.

In traditional Jewish law, if a cremation of a Jewish person does take place, the ashes may not be buried in a Jewish cemetery. Some cemeteries will allow burial of ashes.

Jewish law requires no mourning for the cremated. Shiva is not observed and Kaddish is not recited for them. Those who are cremated are considered by Jewish tradition to have abandoned, unalterably, all of Jewish law and therefore, to have surrendered their rights to posthumous honor. More liberal Jews will observe full mourning rites, even when cremation does occur.

EUTHANASIA

Euthanasia, from the Greek meaning "beautiful death" and sometimes referred to as mercy killing, was a term coined by Sir Thomas More to describe the painless and merciful killing of incurables. Confrontation with this issue immediately provokes moral, religious, and legal reverberations, striking at basic human and social values. The subject calls into question the inviolability and sacredness of life and the right of a man himself, his close relatives, or a physician to determine when life should end. The emotional problem arises as to the value of a life carried on in pain, or in a state of unconsciousness. Though rarely overtly expressed, financial considerations are also important, when an obvious incurable is kept alive by drugs or artificial means.

An additional question concerns the right to die. One's right to live is unquestioned, but does one also have the right to die? Is that right violated when a person is kept alive unnecessarily under excruciating or degrading circumstance?

Most religious groups believe that life and death are Divine gifts, and that a person should not usurp the will of God. Life ends when God decrees. Though one may not understand unnecessary suffering and may want to terminate it, to do so is not given to man.

This is the basic position of Judaism which has as its underlying premise the affirmation that God, and not man, is the final arbiter in life.

Euthanasia has been discussed in the Bible, the Talmud and the Jewish law codes for many centuries. Here are some selections which serve as the bases of rabbinic decisions:

From the Bible

1. Whoever sheds the blood of man, by man shall his blood be shed, for in His image did God make man. (Genesis 9:6)

2. When a man schemes against another and kills him treacherously, you shall take him from My very altar to be put to death. (Exodus 21:14)

3. You shall not commit murder. (Exodus 20:13)

4. The spirit of God has made me and the breath of the Almighty give me life. (Job 33:4)

5. Behold, all souls are Mine. (Ezekiel 18:4)

From the Talmud

1. A dying man is considered the same as a living man in every respect ... He may inherit property and he may bequeath prop-

erty. If a limb is severed from his body, it is regarded as a limb severed from a living person, if flesh, as flesh from a living person . . . all this applies to the moment he dies . . . He may not be stirred, nor may he be washed, and he should not be laid on salt or sand, until the moment he dies . . . His eyes may not be closed. Whosoever touches him or stirs him sheds blood. (Talmud, Semachot 1:1–2)

2. Therefore, was man created alone, to teach you that whosoever destroys a single soul, Scripture imputes guilt to him as though he had destroyed a complete world. (Talmud, Sanhedrin 37a)

3. One may not close the eyes of corpse on the Sabbath, nor on week days when he is about to die, and he who closes the eyes of a dying person when the soul is still departing (such an act promoting death) is a murderer. (Talmud, Shabbat 151b)

Codes and Commentaries

1. It seems to me that there are times when it is necessary to pray that he die, as for example, if the sick person suffers greatly and it is in any case impossible for him to continue living much longer. (Rabbi Nissim Gerondi commenting on Nedarim 40a)

2. Whoever kills a healthy person and whoever kills a sick person who is dying, though his or her death is imminent, are all guilty of murder. (Maimonides, Laws of Murder, 2:6)

3. One who is dying is for all intents and purposes considered to be alive. Hence, nothing must be done to hasten death . . . (Code of Jewish Law, Yoreh Deah, 339:1)

If one sifts through these sources, one can see that rabbinic opinion condemns any active intervention that could shorten a person's life.

The issue becomes clouded, however, because postponing death unnecessarily is also prohibited and even traditional authorities do not all agree over what constitutes active cessation of life.

Orthodox opinion today seems to suggest that we are not required to attach any life-prolonging devices to a terminally ill patient, but may not remove them once attached. Some Conservative authorities seem to suggest that we may remove such devices and allow nature to take its course. Reform Judaism and some Reconstructionist authorities hold that we are forbidden to prolong a life that has been reduced to the status of a "vegetable."

Rabbinic legal opinions continue to be developed and modified, and one will wish to check with one's own local rabbi regarding questions related to euthanasia.

AMPUTATED LIMBS

The blood and the limbs of an individual are considered by Jewish law to be a part of the human being. As such, they require burial. If the deceased was found with severed limbs, they must be buried with him or her.

If limbs were amputated during one's lifetime, they require burial in the person's future gravesite. If that person does not own a plot as yet, or if he or she is squeamish in this regard, it should be buried in a separate plot, preferably near the graves of members of his or her family. The limbs are cleansed and placed in the earth, and no observance of mourning is necessary.

ORGAN DONATIONS

The twentieth century has seen a medical revolution in organ donations. In 1905 the first cornea graft took place, and since then transplants of many kinds have occurred. In 1967, the first human heart transplant operation was performed in Capetown, South Africa.

The whole area of organ donations, with its religious, moral, and legal ramifications, has proven to be more problematic than the first corneal operation would have led people to suspect. The issue of human dissection, mutilation, the rights of the living as they balance against rights of the dead, come to the fore, as do the related issues of autopsy and post mortem.

What does Judaism specifically have to say about transplants? May a person will various organs for scientific research? Does a person have the moral right to give his body part, or part of it during his life, thereby threatening his own existence or shortening its length?

Jewish sources do provide some basis for an understanding of this whole issue. These have mainly to do with the value given to life and the treatment of death.

Judaism maintains unequivocally that the life of a human being. is of infinite value, and any reduction of that life, in any way, by human hands, constitutes homicide, no matter what the condition, age or circumstance. The value of human life is so absolute that, for its sake, Judaism suspends every law, of whatever kind, except the primary crimes of incest, idolatry, and murder. Related to this emphasis on the high value placed upon life is the necessity, if organ transplants are to be carried out, to ascertain as nearly as possible the exact moment of death.

Other rabbinic concerns include the laws related to preservation and dignity of the body versus the laws related to "pikuach nefesh"—the saving of a person's life.

While the donation of limbs seems to be contrary to traditional Jewish law (and subject to a more liberal interpretation by liberal authorities), the donation of organs continues today to remain under constant rabbinic debate. Such donations should be discussed in depth with a rabbinic authority. However, organ donation is generally encouraged by all branches of Judaism as a means of saving and extending life.

AUTOPSIES

The issue of autopsy and dissection of the body is in a sense related to the question of organ transplants. Even though the motive of medical study is a worthy one, Jewish tradition held that an autopsy violated the higher principle—that of mutilating the body of the deceased. Judaism has always demanded respect for the total person—his body and his soul.

Although opinions are not clear-cut, the general position in the Orthodox world is that autopsies to ascertain the cause of death are forbidden unless the civil authorities order otherwise. In the same way, dissection is regarded as a desecration of the human body. Most Conservative, Reform, and Reconstructionist authorities hold that autopsies may be performed if they will directly affect a person suffering from the same disease or it can be clearly demonstrated that they will expand our general medical knowledge.

EXHUMATION

Judaism finds the idea of moving a body from one grave to another reprehensible. However, there are situations which require exhumation and reburial. They are:

1. To transfer the body to a grave in the State of Israel.

2. To transfer the body from a non-Jewish cemetery to a Jewish one.

3. If a cemetery is undermined by excessive water (due to flooding).

4. If civil law requires investigation into the cause of death. The vacated grave may be used for burial by another person.

SEVEN

Helping Children Understand Death

A child can stand tears, but not treachery, sorrow, but not deceit.

—(Joshua Liebman)

Our society abounds with role models concerning the happier life cycle events, but it is sadly lacking in realistic guidelines for grief. Children, especially younger ones who may not yet have the language to express their experience of grief, are dependent upon their parents and other adults. Often times, parents try to protect their children from the pain of grief, but this is usually impossible. As Rabbi Earl Grollman, a leading teacher in the Jewish way of death and dying has stated, "Grief is the price we pay for having loved." If a child has loved, that child will grieve. Any efforts to protect a child from the pain of loss and the expression of that pain may inhibit a healthy, necessary expression.

A child's ability to understand the meaning of death and loss is dependent on his or her cognitive development, life experiences, and view of the world and his or her place in it.

CHILDREN'S UNDERSTANDING OF DEATH

Children are much more aware of death than one may realize. That moment when life no longer exists often confronts them at an early age, with the death of a pet, or a funeral procession that passes by. However, although children may be familiar with the words "dead" and "died," their comprehension of these terms are likely quite different than that of adults.

A child of two years of age can sense loss and suffer the feelings that go with that loss, but is not likely to comprehend death in an intellectual sense. A parent can respond to a child's feelings, but explanations, even if possible, are likely to be of little value at this age. Children of ages three and four, however, have been exposed to the death of plants, insects, and animals. At this age they tend to think of death as a temporary condition and view it as a separation.

Between the ages of five and nine, children are much better able to understand the meaning of physical death because of their developing life experiences. At this age they may begin to worry about the non existence of people close to them, and conceive of death as a ghost or a bogeyman.

By the time children are nine or ten, and thereafter, children formulate more realistic conceptions based on biological observances and wider experience. Death is the final end of bodily life.

Most social workers believe that it is important to tell children immediately when a death occurs. If possible, children ought to be told by a parent or someone else close to them. Relaying the news in a familiar environment is also highly recommended.

There is no one proper way to tell a child about a death. Although what is said is significant, how it is said is also very important (i.e. the tone of one's voice, and the like). Children ought not to be overwhelmed with too much detail, and one must be extremely careful to talk about death in a language that is on the comprehension level of the child. Theological abstractions and detailed explanations ought to be avoided, so that death will not be linked to sin or divine punishment. Myths and fairy tales that will later have to be rejected, such as that grandpa is sleeping or that grandma went away on a long trip, ought to be avoided.

Children should be allowed time to express themselves and ask questions, if they should have any. Allowing children to reveal their fears and anxieties is also advisable.

It is also wise to contact one's children's school and inform them of the loss in the family. Otherwise, teachers might not understand any change in behavior that could very well occur as a result of the loss of a loved one.

A good rule of thumb is to speak to children from the heart and from your own belief. Be direct and truthful, always guided by the age of the child. Answer the questions asked, as they are asked. Be supportive and understanding, always encouraging questions and discussion.

ATTENDING THE FUNERAL AND BURIAL

Children should be provided with the opportunity to grieve in their own way. One should not assume that because they do not fully comprehend what's going on, they do not understand at all. In the face of death, we all need to be reminded of the promise of life which is present in front of us in the faces of children. As they grow older, they may be thankful for the opportunity that was provided to them, since their memories of the deceased fade over time.

A child who wants to attend the funeral should be permitted to do so. One ought to take one's cue from one's child. If a child is frightened, it would be best to arrange appropriate child care. In any case, the rabbi should sit down with children prior to the funeral and explain what will take place during the funeral. The child also needs a chance to say goodbye.

In Judaism, accompanying the dead to the grave is considered one of the highest forms of loving-kindness. One should not assume that the burial is too traumatic for children. Explaining to them in detail the procedure at the cemetery, one can then consult them as to their wishes and desires. Children's attendance at the cemetery may help them learn the importance of leave-taking.

HELPING CHILDREN WORK THROUGH GRIEF

The following are some helpful tips (as culled from the literature on helping children understand death) to assist in helping a child work through his or her grief.

1. Encourage a child to talk about the deceased and be made to feel that it is acceptable to express negative as well as positive feelings.

2. Do not be afraid of causing tears and in a hurry to stop the flow when it starts.

3. Talk about past events involving the deceased.

4. Reassure the child that he or she had nothing to do with causing the death of the loved one.

5. Be certain to express to your children your own emotions of grief.

EIGHT

WHAT HAPPENS AFTER I DIE?

Blessed are You, O God, who planted eternal life in our midst.

—(Torah Blessing)

THE WORLD BEYOND THE GRAVE

Jews and Judaism have always been more concerned with this world than that of the next, and have concentrated on the performance of good deeds to perfect the world in which we now live. Belief in an afterlife was little pronounced in the early biblical period. During the rabbinic period, however, it began to assume a much more prominent place in Jewish faith. Basically, there were two ideas, originally quite separate, that had been combined by the time of the rabbis: the resurrection of the dead ("techiyat ha-metim") and the immortality of the soul. According to the original resurrection doctrine, when a person dies, that person is truly dead. That person's soul is also dead, until after the age of the Messiah, when it is again reunited with one's body when the latter is raised from the grave.

According to the doctrine of the immortality of the soul, in its original form, the body dies and is permanently lost but the soul lives on forever after the death of the body. Eventually, when the two ideas were combined, the doctrine ran that when a person dies, that person's soul lives on in Heaven until the time of resurrection when soul and body are united.

Orthodox Judaism still accepts the combined beliefs. Reform Judaism rejects the idea of resurrection. Some Conservative, Reform and Reconstructionist Judaism may understand the Messianic idea in more abstract terms. Thus there are prayers in the traditional liturgy both for the repose of the souls of the departed "under the wings of the Divine Presence" and references in the prayers of the resurrection of the dead. The following Sabbath morning hymn expresses the traditional view:

> There is none to be compared with You, neither is there any beside You; there is none but You; who is like unto You? There is none to be compared to You, Adonai our God, in this world, neither is there any beside You, O our Sovereign, for the life of the world to come; there is none but You, O our Redeemer, for the days of the Messiah, neither is there any like unto You, O our Savior, for the resurrection of the dead. (Nishmat Kol Chai)

Here the term "world to come" ("olam haba") clearly refers to the immortality of the soul. On the other hand, the prayer recited during the Grace after the Meals: "May the All-merciful make us worthy of the days of the Messiah, and of the life of the world to come" can only refer to the resurrection of the dead.

IDEAS ABOUT LIFE AFTER DEATH

There are a variety of ideas about the meaning of life after death, immortality, and the various forms that it takes. Following is a summary of some of the ways in which Jewish people have and continue to conceive of immortality today.

Influence through Family

In recording King David's death, the Bible states: "And David slept with his fathers" (I Kings 2:10) The sages wanted to know why the Bible did not simply state "and he died"? The sages answered their own question by asserting that David was survived by a son who followed the good ways of his father's life, continuing his father's noble deeds. Therefore it would not be said that David was really David, for he lived on through the good deeds of his son.

In this form of immortality, we live on through the life of our family and ancestors. This is just another way of saying that we live in and through our children. This naturalistic view posits that the eternal life occurs biologically through the children that we bring into this world.

Immortality through Influence

When we have influenced others to the point that they fashion themselves after us and continue to use us as a role model, this kind of eternal significance is itself a form of immortality.

Influence through Creative Works

Our work can outlast our life. This notion of immortality, based upon influences through our life's work, is suggested by these words of the Talmud: "Whoever has a law mentioned in his name in this world, his lips whisper in the grave" (Talmud Sanhedrin 90a). It is also expressed in this Midrash from Genesis Rabbah 32:10: "We need not erect monuments to the righteous. Their deeds are their monuments."

Influence through Memory

Judaism has always coveted the gift of memory. Abraham Joshua Heschel once wrote that the essence of Jewish religious thinking lies in the ability to articulate a memory. The philosopher Martin Buber once said that the Jews are a community by virtue of historic memory, and are held together by common remembering. In this form of memory, people live on in the memory of those who knew and loved them. Simply remembering people that we admired gives them an aspect of eternity.

Reincarnation

The idea that a soul enters another living entity after the death of its body has intrigued people for centuries. It appears prominently in Hinduism, in the burial customs of many tribes in Africa, in ancient Greek philosophy, and in Judaism, primarily among mystics and Hasidim.

In Hebrew, the technical term for this idea is "gilgul neshamot"— the turning of souls. Mystics who embrace a belief in reincarnation posit that souls have an independent life, existing before and after the death of the body. The soul, they say, joins the body at an appropriate time, remains with it for a specified period, then takes leave of the body about the time of death, prepared to assume its next assignment in the physical world. A soul can return again and again in different bodies, and the ways in which it conducts itself in each reincarnation determines its ascent or descent in its next visit.

Mystics often use reincarnation to explain odd or unusual occurrences of human characteristics. For example, if a person seems to behave like an animal, a kabbalist might well conclude that such a person is carrying the soul of a beast.

Mystics describe three types of reincarnation: "gilgul," "ibbur," and "dybbuk." Gilgul takes place during pregnancy, ibbur (impregnation) occurs when an "old" soul enters the body of another individual at any time during its lifetime. The soul dwells in a new body for a limited period of time and performs certain acts. Finally, when an evil soul enters a person, causing mental illness and a severe change in personality, the invading soul is called a dybbuk (clinging soul). In order to eradicate such a soul, an exorcism must be performed. Kabbalistic literature is filled with stories of exorcisms and even describes the procedures with great detail.

Resurrection

People of many faiths believe that in the distant future the dead will be resurrected, coming back to life. According to the dominant rabbinic view, physical resurrection of the dead would take place at the end of time after the arrival of the Messiah. Rabbi Elazar HaKappar taught: "They that are born are destined to die. And the dead are destined to be brought to life again. The living [i.e. the resurrected] are destined after death to be judged" (Pirkei Avot 4:28).

The rabbis maintained that both body and soul would be brought back to life and jointly subjected to final judgment. Though most Reform and Reconstructionist Jews have set aside a belief in bodily resurrection, for more traditionally minded Jews, a belief in resurrection continues to radiate great hope today.

Rationalist View

Maimonides, the medieval philosopher, proposed, in contrast to the mystics, that in as much as God is pure intelligence, one's godlike qualities reside in our intellects. Therefore, to the extent that we develop our intelligence and reach the knowledge of eternal truth, to that extent we achieve immortality.

Clearly Judaism has posited many different conceptions of immortality. But all of these options are based upon one fundamental concept: In Judaism, God is just and we are all responsible for our actions in this life. Even if a person led an uncaring life, God may still find some small kind deed or some small act of repentance that will suffice for entrance into the world to come.

The basic question, no matter what view of immortality resembles your own, always remains the same: How did you live your life? This thought is wonderfully described in a most beautiful Midrash commenting on the verse in the Book of Psalms 118:17 "open the gates of righteousness for me."

> At the time of judgment in the Future World everyone will be asked, "What was your occupation?" If the person answers, "I used to feed the hungry," they will say to him, "This is God's gate; you who fed the hungry may enter." "I used to give water to those who were thirsty"—they will say to him, "This is God's gate. You who gave water to those who were thirsty may enter." "I used to clothe the naked"—they will say to him, "This is God's gate; you who clothed the naked may enter." . . . and similarly with those who raised orphans, and who performed the mitzvah of tzedakah, and who performed acts of caring, loving-kindness.

NINE

NOTABLE QUOTATIONS AND RABBINIC TALES ON DEATH AND DYING IN JEWISH TRADITION

BURYING THE DEAD AND COMFORTING THE MOURNERS

1. In Judaism, there are a variety of acts of kindness that one can perform for the deceased. This Midrash explains the meaning of the phrase "steadfast loyalty" to refer to an act of kindness that one performs for another after that person has died.

> "Act in steadfast loyalty to me . . . carry me out of Egypt, and bury me" (Genesis 47:29–30). Is there such a thing as loyalty that is not steadfast? No, but what Jacob said to Joseph was: If *after* my death you act in loyalty toward me, that will be "steadfast loyalty."
>
> Why did Jacob speak this way? He spoke in refutation of the cynical proverb "When your friend's son dies, give your friend sympathy; when your friend himself dies, be on your way" (Genesis Rabbah 96:5).

2. The following Talmudic story explains various opinions concerning one's responsibility to close the eyes of the deceased.

> Our rabbis taught: One who closes the eyes of a dying person at the point of death is a murderer, as may be understood by analogy with a lamp that is flickering out; if one presses one's finger upon it, the lamp goes out at once.
>
> We have been taught that Rabban Simeon ben Gamaliel said: One who wishes the eyes of a dead person to close should blow wine into his nostrils, apply oil between his eyelids, or take hold of his two big toes, and the eyes will close of themselves. (Talmud Shabbat 152b).

3. This Talmudic passage discusses the biblical injunction that one must be buried the same day as one's death, and under what circumstance delay in burial to honor the deceased may occur.

> Rabbi Yochanan said in the name of Rabbi Simeon ben Yochai: What is the proof that he who keeps his dead unburied overnight transgresses a negative mitzvah? The verse "his body shall not remain overnight . . . You shall surely bury him the same day" (Deuteronomy 21:23).
>
> If the relative keeps the body overnight to honor the deceased—to have his death made known in nearby towns, to bring professional women mourners for him, or to obtain for him a casket and shrouds—he violates no precept, for all that he does [even though it delays the burial] is done for the honor of the deceased (Talmud Sanhedrin 46b–47a)

4. It is a religious obligation to bury the dead. The following Talmudic passage discusses the various sources of this mitzvah. The ancient Persians regarded burial as a desecration of the

earth. Thus included in this Talmudic passage is the opinion of the Persian King Shapur who came into contact with many rabbinic thinkers. He was opposed to burial of corpses in the ground, and sought to demolish Jewish arguments that in ground burial is a requirement.

Rabbi Yochanan said in the name of Rabbi Simeon ben Yochai: Where in the Torah is burial of the dead alluded to as a precept? In the verse "Bury, you shall bury him" (Deuteronomy 21:23).

King Shapur asked Rabbi Hama: From where in the Torah is the obligation to bury the dead derived? Rav Hama remained silent, saying nothing in reply. Upon hearing about this incident, Rabbi Acha bar Jacob said, "The world is given over into the hands of fools." Rav Hama should have cited, "Bury . . . him."

[King Shapur might have responded]: Perhaps the words imply that the body must be placed in a casket?

Rabbi Hama should have quoted the complete verse: "Bury, you shall bury him" [the repetition of the word "bury" indicates in-ground burial] (Talmud Sanhedrin 46b).

5. This passage discusses one's Jewish obligation related to the discovery of an unidentified body.

When a man finds an unidentified body, he should attend to its needs and bury it in the place where it was found. Rabbi Akiva said: This is how my ministry to the sages began. Once, while walking on a road, I found a slain man. I carried him a distance of four *mil* to a burial place, where I buried him. When I came to Rabbi Eliezer and Rabbi Joshua, I told them what had happened. They said to me, "Every step you took is deemed against you as though you had shed blood." Then I said to myself, reasoning from the minor to the major: If I incurred sin when I thought to do good, how much more sin would I have incurred had I not thought to do good. Henceforth I did not deviate from ministering to the sages (Jerusalem Talmud Nazir 7:1).

6. This teaching discusses whether it is permissible to interrupt one's study (a sacred duty in Judaism) to attend a funeral procession.

Our rabbis taught: One may interrupt the study of Torah to attend a funeral procession. It is said of Rabbi Judah bar Ilai that he would interrupt the study of Torah to attend a funeral procession, but only when there were not enough people in the procession. When there are enough, study may not be interrupted. How many are enough? Rabbi Samuel bar Ini said in the name of Rav: Twelve thousand men and six thousand trumpeters. Ulla said: As many as would form a continuous line from the city gate to the grave. However, Rav Sheshet (some say Rabbi Yochanan) said: The interruption of Torah study requires as many to be present as there were when it was given. Since the Torah was given in the presence of sixty myriads, so it can be interrupted only if sixty myriads are present.

When may study be interrupted by the presence of sixty myriads? At the funeral of one who read Bible and recited Mishnah. But at a funeral of one who taught Bible and Mishnah, there is no limit (Talmud Ketubot 17a).

7. In the following story we learn the rabbinic lesson that teaches how bones of the deceased are to be treated and transported from one place to another for burial.

Our masters taught: A man who transports bones from one place to another should not put them in a saddlebag, place the bag on his donkey's back, and then sit on it, because this is a disrespectful way of treating them. But if he is afraid of heathens or robbers, he may do so. And the rule laid down for bones applies also to a Torah scroll (Talmud Berachot 18b).

8. This story provides rabbinic advice concerning the appropriateness of burial of a righteous person next to a wicked one.

Rabbi Acha bar Hanina said: A wicked person should not be buried next to a righteous one; and just as a wicked person should not be buried next to a righteous one, so is a grossly wicked person not to be buried next to one who is mildly wicked (Talmud Sanhedrin 47a).

9. The following story provides advice regard the appropriateness of taking sanctified Jewish ritual objects into a cemetery.

We have been taught: A person should not walk about in a cemetery with tefillin on one's head, nor read from a Torah scroll held on one's arm. If one does this, one shows no concern for the assertion "He that mocks the poor (i.e. the dead) blasphemes his Maker" (Proverbs 17:5; Talmud Berachot 18a).

10. Should one be allowed to make injurious remarks about the deceased? This talmudic citation presents us with several points of view.

Rabbi Isaac said: if one makes harmful remarks about the deceased, it is like making remarks about a stone. Some say the reason is that they do not know; others say that they know but do not care. But is that really so? Did not Rav Papa tell of a certain person who made derogatory remarks about Samuel while following his bier, and a log fell from the roof and cracked that man's skull? A disciple of the wise [such as Samuel] is different, because the Holy One demands the deference due him (Talmud Berachot 19a).

11. The following Talmudic tale describes the importance of the lack of ostentation in the burial rite of Jewish person. All are to be buried in simple linen shrouds, thus reinforcing the concept of democracy in death. Both rich and poor are buried alike in these unostentatious garments.

> At one time, providing decent burial was more burdensome for the family of the deceased than even his death, so they would leave the body and run away, until Rabbi Gamaliel came and prescribed a simple style for himself. He was carried out in an inexpensive linen shroud. Thereafter all people followed his practice by carrying out their dead in inexpensive linen shrouds.
>
> Rav Papa added: And now it is the practice to take out the dead even in a shroud of rough cloth worth no more than a "zuz" (Talmud Ketubot 8b)

12. The following Talmudic tale illustrates again the democracy in death. Both rich and poor alike are to receive the same treatment, so that a poorer family will not feel humiliated.

> Our rabbis taught: Formerly the faces of the rich were left uncovered, while the faces of the poor, which during years of drought had turned dark, were covered; understandably, the poor felt humiliated. In deference to their feelings, it was instituted that everybody's face should be covered.
>
> Formerly, the rich were carried out for burial on a state bed, and the poor on a plain bier; understandably, the poor felt humiliated. In deference to their feelings, it was instituted that all should be taken out on a plain bier.
>
> Formerly, a perfuming pan was placed under those who died of disease of the bowels. Understandably, the living sufferers from such disease felt humiliated. In deference to their feelings, it was enacted that such a pan should be set under all who died (Talmud Moed Katan, 27a–27b).

13. The following Talmudic tale speaks about the institution of the custom of mourners passing down an aisle surrounded by people who are standing upon taking leave of the cemetery.

> Our rabbis taught: Formerly the mourners used to stand still, while all the people passed in front of them. But there were two families in Jerusalem who argued with one another, each insisting: "We shall pass first." So the rabbis laid down the rule that the people should remain standing, and the mourners pass in front of them (Talmud Sanhedrin 19a).

14. The following Talmudic story describes the ancient custom of drinking ten cups of wine in the house of the bereaved.

> We have been taught: The rabbis instituted that ten cups of wine be drunk in the house of a mourner: three before the meal, in order to open the small bowels; three during the meal, in order to dissolve the food in the bowels; and four after the meal—one corresponding to "who feeds" [i.e. first blessing of Grace after the meal], one corresponding to the "blessing for the land" [second blessing of Grace after meal], one corresponding to "who rebuilds Jerusalem" [third blessing of Grace after meal] and one corresponding to "who is good and does good." Then the rabbis added another four cups: one in honor of the town officers, one in honor of the town leaders, one in honor of the Temple and one in honor of Rabban Gamaliel. But when people began to drink so much that they became intoxicated, the practice of drinking the original number of ten cups was restored (Talmud Ketubot 8b).

15. The following brief instruction speaks about the importance to God of one's tears that flow in honor of a virtuous person.

> The rabbis said in the name of Bar Kappara: When one sheds tears at the death of a virtuous person, the Holy One counts

them and places them in His treasure house (Talmud Shabbat 105b).

16. This Talmudic statement illustrates the custom of the playing of flutes and the use of professional mourners at a funeral in ancient rabbinic times.

Rabbi Judah said: Even the poorest person in Israel should provide for his wife's funeral not less than two flutes and at least one professional female mourner (Talmud Ketubot 46b).

17. This Talmudic passage records the ancient custom in the city of Jerusalem and in Judea of saying things about the deceased while the casket is moving in its procession.

In Jerusalem they used to walk in front of the bier reciting the things a deceased person had done, while in Judea they used to recite behind the casket the things he had done. For in Jerusalem they recited in front of the casket only the things he had actually done, while behind the casket they recited the things he had done as well as the things he had not done. However, in Judea they recited in front of the bier the things he had done as well as things he had not done, but those who followed the bier did not respond to all things recited, limiting themselves to only things he had done (Talmud Semachot 3).

18. This rabbinic story details appropriate things to say to the mourners when a death has occurred.

It once happened that a child of Rabbi Chiyya bar Abba, the teacher of Resh Lakish's son, died. The first day of Rabbi Chiyya's mourning, Resh Lakish did not go to him. The next day, Resh Lakish took along Judah bar Nachmani, his interpreter, and said to him, "Rise and say something appropriate to the death of the child." Judah began his remarks with the verse "When God saw that He was spurned, God moved in anger against a man's sons and daughters" (Deuteronomy 32:19). When there is a generation in which fathers spurn the Holy One, God moves in anger against their sons and daughters, so that they die young. Did Judah, invited to comfort Rabbi Chiyya, mean to add to his grief by speaking this way? On the contrary, he meant: "You Rabbi Chiyya are so important as to be punished by the loss of your child for the shortcomings of your generation."

Then Resh Lakish said to Judah, "Rise and say something suitable to the praise of the Holy One." Judah began his discourse by saying, "O God, who is great in the abundance of His greatness, mighty and strong in the multitude of awesome deeds, who with His word revives the dead, who does great things that are unsearchable and wondrous works without number. Blessed are You, O God, who revives the dead."

Then Resh Lakish said to Judah, "Rise and say something appropriate to the mourners." Judah began his discourse by saying, "Our brethren, worn out and crushed by this bereavement, set your hearts to consider this: your experiences is one that abides forever; it is a path trodden even since the six days of creation. Many have drunk this cup of sorrow; many will drink. Like the drinking of the former, so will be the drinking of the latter. Our brethren, may the Lord of consolations comfort you. Blessed be God who comforts the mourners."

Then Resh Lakish said to Judah, "Rise and say something appropriate to those who comfort mourners." Judah began his discourse by saying, "Our brethren, bestowers of loving-kindness, children of bestowers of loving-kindness, who hold fast to the covenant of Abraham our father, our brethren, may the Lord of requital give you your reward. Blessed are You, O Lord, who gives the reward due."

Resh Lakish then said to Judah, "Rise and say something capable of consoling all of Israel." Judah began his discourse by saying, "Lord of the universe, redeem and save, deliver and rescue Your people Israel from pestilence and from the sword, from plundering and from the blast, from mildew and from all kinds of calamities stirring up to overwhelm the world. Even before we call, may You answer. Blessed are You who stays the plague" (Talmud Ketubot 8b).

19. In this Talmudic story we learn of the rabbinic advice concerning excessive mourning for the deceased.

"Weep not for the dead, neither bemoan him" (Jeremiah 23:10) "Weep not for the dead" in excess, "neither bemoan him" beyond measure. What does this mean? Three days of weeping, seven for lamenting, and thirty days for refraining from wearing pressed clothes and from trimming the hair. "From then on," says the Holy One, "you are not expected to be more compassionate to him than I" (Talmud Moed Katan, 27b).

WORLD TO COME

These quotations and rabbinic stories relate to views of the World to Come.

1. This rabbinic story explains the meaning of the "day of kissing."

"You protect my head on the day of kissing" (Psalm 140:8)—the day when the two worlds kiss each other, the day a man leaves this world and enters the world to come (Jerusalem Talmud Yevamot 15:2).

2. The following is Rav's description of the world to come and what one will find in it.

Rav had a favorite saying: The world to come is not at all like this world. In the world to come, there is no eating, no drinking, no procreation, no commerce, no envy, no hatred, no rivalry; the righteous sit with crowns on their heads and enjoy the radiance of God (Talmud Berachot 17a).

3. The following is Rabbi Joshua ben Levi's view of the world to come.

Rabbi Joshua ben Levi said: In the world to come, the Holy One will have each righteous person inherit three hundred and ten worlds, as intimated in the verse "That I may cause those that love Me to inherit "yesh" [whose Hebrew letters "yud" (ten) and "shin" (three hundred) add up to three hundred and ten]" (Proverbs 8:21).

4. The following is Rabbah's view of the world to come.

Rabbah said in the name of Rabbi Yochanan: In time to come, the Holy One will set up seven canopies for each and every righteous person.

"Smoke, and the shining of fire ... for each glory shall be a canopy" (Isaiah 4:4). The verse implies that the canopy the Holy One makes for each and every righteous man will be in keeping with the glory that is to be accorded him (Talmud Baba Batra 75a).

5. The following explains the world to come that righteous people are afforded.

"When man goes to his own long habitation" (Ecclesiastes 12:5) Rabbi Isaac said: The verse implies that every righteous person is given a habitation as befits the honor due him. The matter may be understood by the parable of a king who enters a city with his servants. When they enter, all of them enter through the same gate. But when they lodge overnight, each one is given a habitation in keeping with the honor due him (Talmud Shabbat 152a).

6. In this rabbinic teaching we learn the relationship between angels and souls of the wicked and the righteous in the world to come.

We have been taught that Rabbi Eliezer said: The souls of the righteous are treasured under the throne of glory, as is said, "The soul of my lord shall be treasured in the treasury of life" (I Samuel 25:29). But the soul of the wicked is tied up and tossed about. One angel stands at one end of the world and another angel stands at the other end of the world, and they sling the souls of the wicked to each other, as is said, "The souls of your enemies, them shall God sling out, as from the hollow of a sling" (Talmud Shabbat 152b).

7. In this Talmudic passage we learn what happens to Rabbi Joseph's spirit as it leaves his body for some time, (and flys to the world to come) only to return to him.

Rabbi Joseph son of Rabbi Joshua ben Levi became ill, and his spirit flew away. After his spirit returned to him, his father asked him, "What did you see? He replied, "I saw a world turned upside down—the people high up here were moved down, and the lowly here were moved up." Rabbi Joshua: "My son, you saw a world in which right is made clear. But what of you and me—where were we placed?" "Just as we are esteemed here, so were we esteemed there. I also heard them say, 'Happy is he who comes here with his learning in hand.' I also heard them say, 'They who were martyred by the Roman government—no person is allowed to stand within their compartments' " (Talmud Pesachim 50a).

8. This rabbinic passage tells of those who have a portion in the world to come.

All Israel have a portion in the world to come, as is said, "Your people are all righteous. They shall inherit the world that is forever: the branch of My planting, the work of My hands, wherein I glory" (Isaiah 60:21).

Three kings and four commoners have no portion in the world to come. The three kings are Jeroboam, Ahab, and Manasseh. Rabbi Judah, however, said: Manasseh has a portion in the world to come, for it is said, "And he prayed unto God . . . and God listened to his supplication and brought him to Jerusalem into his kingdom" (II Chronicles 33:13). The sages retorted to Rabbi Judah: God brought him to his kingdom, but not to life in the world to come. The four commoners: Balaam Doeg, Achitophel and Gehazi.

Who enumerated them? The Men of the Great Assembly.

The Men of the Great Assembly were about to include one more, Solomon, but the apparition of his father's likeness came and prostrated itself before them. However, they ignored it. Then a fire came down from heaven and licked about their benches, but they ignored it also. At that, a divine voice cried out to them, "Do you see a man diligent in his business? He shall stand with kings; he shall not stand with mean men" (Proverbs 22:29). He who gave precedence to the building of My house over his and built My house in seven years but his own in thirteen, "he shall stand with kings; he shall not stand with mean men." But they ignored that also. Then the divine voice cried out, "Shall his recompense be as you will . . . Will you choose, and not I?" (Job 34:33).

They who look for the inherent meaning of Scripture maintain: All the aforementioned will enter the world to come (Talmud Sanhedrin 90a and 104b).

THE GARDEN OF EDEN AND GEHENNA

1. The following is a rabbinic portrayal of paradise—the Garden of Eden as seen through the eyes of Rabbi Joshua ben Levi.

Rabbi Joshua ben Levi said: there are two gates of chalcedony in the Garden of Eden, and around them are sixty myriads of ministering angels, the radiance of the countenance of each of whom shines like the splendor of the firmament. When a righteous person comes to them, they remove from him the garments in which he abode in the grave and clothe him in eight garments of clouds of glory. They put two crowns on his head, one of precious stones and pearls, and the other of Parvaim gold. They place eight myrtles in his hand and chant praise before him, saying, "Go, eat your bread with joy" (Ecclesiastes 9:7). Then they bring him to a place of waterbrooks encompassed by eight hundred species of roses and myrtles. Each and every righteous person is given a canopy in keeping with the honor due him. Out of it flow four rivers, one of milk, one of wine, one of balsam and one of honey. Each and every canopy has above it a vine of gold in which thirty pearls are set, and the brightness of each shines like the brightness of the planet Venus. Each and every canopy has in it a table made of precious stones and pearls. Sixty angels stand at the head of each and every righteous man, and say to him: Come and eat honey in gladness, because you have occupied yourself with Torah, which is likened to honey; and drink the wine kept in its grapes ever since the six days of creation, because you have occupied yourself with Torah, which is likened to wine. The most homely among the angels has a visage like that of Joseph or Rabbi Yochanan.

For the righteous, there is no night. During the night's three watches, each righteous person becomes a child and enters the compartment for little children, where he rejoices the way little children rejoice. During the second watch, each righteous person becomes a young man and enters the compartment of young men, where he rejoices the way young men rejoice. During the third watch, each righteous person becomes an old man and enters the compartment for old men, where he rejoices the way old men rejoice (Yalkut, Bereshit, paragraph 2).

2. Following is another rabbinic description of both the Garden of Eden and Gehenna in which is graphically described God's place and the role of angels.

The Holy One will be seated in the Garden of Eden and expound Scripture with all the righteous seated before Him, all the heavenly household standing on their feet, the sun and the planets at the Holy One's right, and the moon and stars at God's left. The Holy One will be seated and expound a new Torah, which God is to give through the Messiah. When God finishes the lesson, Zerubbabel, son of Shealtiel will stand up on his feet and say, "May God be magnified and hallowed," and his voice will go from world's end to world's end. All the world's inhabitants from one of the world to the other will loudly respond "Amen." Even Israel's wicked and the righteous from among the worshipers of idols still remaining in Gehenna will loudly respond out of Gehenna and say, "Amen." The world will be in such commotion that the sound of their loud response will be heard in the presence of the Holy One, who will ask, "What is this great commotion I hear?" The ministering angels will answer, Master of the Universe, these are the wicked of Israel and the righteous of the nations of the world still in Gehenna, who respond with "Amen" and declare their punishment to be just. Then the mercies of the Holy One will surge up mightily for them, and God will say, "What more am I to do about the judgment imposed on them? The impulse to evil is responsible for what has happened to them."

In that instant, in the presence of all the righteous, the Holy One will take the keys to Gehenna, give them to the angels Michael and Gabriel, and say to them, "God, open the gates of all the Gehennas and bring them up." Immediately, Michael and Gabriel will go with the keys and open the eight thousand gates of Gehenna ... Once a wicked person falls into it, he cannot get up out of it. What will Michael and Gabriel do at that time? They will take hold of the hand of each one of them and bring them up, just like a man who bring his fellow up out of a pit by lifting him with a rope. Then the two angels will stand over them, bathe them, anoint them, heal them of the wounds sustained in Gehenna, clothe them in comely garments, and bring them, thus vested gloriously like priests, before the Holy One and to all the righteous, as it is written, "Like Your priests they will be clothed in righteousness, and Your holy ones will sing for joy." (Psalm 132:9).

When they are about to arrive at the entrance to the Garden of Eden, Michael and Gabriel will come in first to seek permission from the Holy One, who will respond saying, "Allow them to come in, that they may behold My glory." When they come in they will fall on their faces, prostrate themselves before God, and bless and praise the Name of the Holy One (Yalkut, Isaiah, paragraph 429).

3. Following is yet another rabbinic description of Gehenna.

Why is it called Gehenna? Because the sound of the groaning within it goes from world's end to world's end.

There are three gates to Gehenna, one at the sea, another at the wilderness, and the third at inhabited land.

There are five kinds of fire in Gehenna: a fire that eats and drinks, one that drinks but does not eat, one that eats but does not drink, one that neither eats nor drinks, and a fire that eats fire. In Gehenna there are coals as big as mountains, coals as small as hills, coals the size of the Salt Sea, and coals that are no larger than big boulders. Also in Gehenna are rivers of pitch and sulphur flowing in boiling suds, continuously boiling and boiling.

The decree upon a wicked man: angels of destruction push him down on his face, and other such angels receive him from them and shove him farther toward the first of Gehenna, which opens its mouth and swallows him. But one who possesses Torah and good deeds and has suffered numerous afflictions is delivered from the judgment of Gehenna, as is said, "Even when I walk through the valley of deepest darkness, I will fear no evil... Your rod and Your staff, they comfort me" [Psalm 23:4] "Your rod" refers to afflictions and "Your staff" to Torah...

Those who go down to Gehenna and are not allowed to come up out of it, are taken every Sabbath eve to two mountains of snow and left there. At the Sabbath's end, an angel goes forth and shoves them along until he returns them to their places in Gehenna. But before leaving, some of them take a handful of snow, which they put in their armpits to keep them cool during the six weekdays. Then the Holy One says to them, "O wicked ones, woe to you, who steal even in Gehenna, as is said, 'Because of the drought and heat they steal the snow waters—they sin even in Sheol' " (Job 24:19).

Throughout twelve months the wicked are reduced to ash, which the wind scatters under the feet of the righteous. After that, their soul returns to them and they go out of Gehenna, their faces as black as the bottom of the pot. They then declare that they deserved the decree of judgment against them, saying, "Rightly You decreed against us. Properly You punished us..." (Massachet Gehinnom, Bet HaMidrash 1:147–149).

4. The following statement is Rabbi Akiba's opinion regarding the length of punishment for the wicked in Gehenna.

Rabbi Akiba used to say: The punishment of the wicked in Gehenna lasts no more than twelve months (Talmud Eduyot 2:10).

ANGEL OF DEATH

1. Stories abound concerning the angel of death. This is one tale that attempts to describe the angel. If you know what the angel looks like, maybe you can avoid it when you see it, goes the logic.

> The Angel of Death is said to be full of eyes. When the hour comes for a sick person to die, the Angel of Death positions itself above the head of the sick person with a sword drawn in the angel's hand. On the sword, a drop of gall dangles precariously. When the sick person sees the Angel of Death, the sick person trembles with fear and opens his or her mouth. At that point, the Angel of Death flicks a drop of gall into the sick person's mouth. From that drop, the sick person dies and the face turns green (Talmud Avodah Zarah 20a).

2. Some say that we should have sympathy for the Angel of Death since she is just doing her job, fulfilling her responsibility to the world. And that is when she is happiest.

> There were two Ethiopians, Elihoreph and Ahijah, the sons of Shisha (I Kings 4:3), who served Solomon as scribes. One day, Solomon saw that the Angel of Death was sulking. Solomon said to the angel, "Why are you sulking?" The angel answered, "Because I was supposed to take these two Ethiopians who are sitting here." As a result, Solomon delivered them to the demons in Luz [in order to save their lives]. The Angel of Death has no power there. But as soon as they approached Luz, they died. The next day Solomon saw the Angel of Death, who was very happy. Solomon said to the angel, "Why are you so happy?" The Angel of Death's response was "Because you sent them to a place where I was required to take their lives." Spontaneously, Solomon remarked, "The feet of humans vouch for them; they take a person where that person is supposed to be" (Talmud Sukkah 53a).

3. This rabbinic story suggests that the angel that accompanies the individual into this world is the same one that accompanies the individual out of this world at death.

When a person's turn to die comes, the same angel that assisted her at birth comes and says to her, "Do you recognize me?" The person answers, "Yes," and continues, "why did you come for me today of all days?" So the angel responds, "In order to take you away from this world, for your time to depart has arrived." Instantly the person begins to cry, and her voice is heard from one end of the earth to the other. No creature recognizes her voice except for the rooster. So the person says to the angel, "You removed me from two worlds and placed me in this world. Why then do you want to take me out of this world?" The angel answers, "Did I not tell you that you were created against your will, born against your will, and will have to give an accounting before the Holy Blessed One against your will?" (Tanchuma, Pekudei 3).

4. In this rabbinic tale, Rabbi Shimon ben Chalafta confronts the Angel of Death on his return home from a celebration following the circumcision of a member of his community.

Once Rabbi Shimon ben Chalafta went to a celebration following a circumcision. The boy's parents sponsored the banquet and offered their guests seven-year-old wine to drink. They said to their guests, "We will set aside some of this wine for the wedding feast of our son." The celebration continued until midnight. Rabbi Shimon ben Chalafta, who trusted in his power to fight off demons, left the party at midnight in order to return home.

On his way home, he encountered the Angel of Death but saw something peculiar about it. So he said, "Who are you?" The angel answered, "I am God's messenger." So Rabbi Shimon said, "Why do you refer to yourself that way?" The angel replied, "Because of the way people talk. They say, 'We shall do this and this,' and they do not know when they will be called to die. Those people who just celebrated the circumcision of their children, their turn will come in thirty days."

Rabbi Shimon said, "show me my turn." But the angel replied, "I have no power over you and those like you because the Holy One wants your good deeds and lengthens your and their lives" (Based on Deuteronomy Rabbah 9:1).

DEATH AND BURIAL OF FAMOUS RABBINIC PERSONALITIES

1. Death of Rabbi Akiba: Rabbi Akiba joined his colleagues in a frightful death at the hands of the Romans, but even at his death he was able to fulfill the mitzvot, one of which he had to wait until his death to be able to fulfill.

Akiba was already forty years old when he came to learn Torah. His thirst for Torah could not be quenched even by the Romans, who forbade the study of Torah, declaring that whoever was caught studying or teaching Torah would be put to death. Unafraid, Akiba continued to teach his students in public.

But eventually he was caught. When he was taken out to be executed, Akiba was ready to recite the Shema. The Romans planned a torturous death for him, combing the flesh from his body with combs of iron, shredding his flesh until he died. But Akiba did not care about the pain. His disciples wondered how their teacher could endure such pain and still concentrate on holy things. Even at the end of his life, Akiba taught them: "All my life I was distressed when I declared my love for God '*bechol nafshecha.*' I am supposed to declare my love with all my soul, which means even if God takes away your life from you. I always wondered if I would be able to actually fulfill this mitzvah. And now, I finally have the opportunity to do so. How can I do anything else?" And putting what strength he had in his body, he passionately uttered the word "echad" (one), and his soul returned to the Creator with the purity with which it had been given him (Talmud Berachot 61b).

2. **Impending Death of Rabbi Zusya: While people often wish they were someone other than themselves, this Hasidic story reminds us that we should try to make something out of our lives with whatever unique talents God gave us. If we can live our lives knowing we have done just that, there is nothing to fear at the end of our days.**

When the students of Zusya approached their dying teacher, he whispered to them, "My students, I am very afraid."

His students were shocked and responded, "Reb Zusya, did you not always teach us that we should have no fear of dying because God is our Parent and God is filled with kindness and compassion?"

"That's true," replied Zusya, "but that is not why I am so frightened. I am not afraid that when I stand before the Throne of Judgment God will say to me, 'Zusya, why were you not Moses?' because I am not a Moses. And I am not afraid that God will say to me, 'Why were you not an Isaiah?' because I am not an Isaiah. But, my dear students, I am afraid that when God asks me, 'Zusya, why were you not Zusya? Why didn't you live up to the best that Zusya could have been?' I am afraid, for what shall I answer?" (Hasidic story).

3. **The Deathbed of Akavya ben Mahalel: This Talmudic story describes the importance of a person's good deeds and how they affect people even after their death.**

When Akavya ben Mahalel was on his deathbed, his son requested, "Father, commend me to your colleagues." Akavya replied, "I will not commend you." His son asked, "Have you found some fault with me?"

His father answered, "No. But your own good deeds will bring you near to them without any commendation, and your own bad deeds will remove you far from them despite any commendation" (Jerusalem Talmud Eduyot 5:7).

4. The Death of Rabbi Yochanan ben Zakkai: This Talmudic story deals with the reason Rabbi Yochanan ben Zakkai cried when he learned of his impending death. The crying resulted from Rabbi Yochanan's not knowing whether the future would bring him to Paradise or Gehinnom.

When Rabbi Yochanan ben Zakkai was very ill, his students visited him. Seeing them, Rabbi Yochanan started to weep. "Lamp of Israel, mighty hammer," they said to him. "Why are you crying?"

Rabbi Yochanan answered, "If I were being led today before a human king, whose anger, if he were angry with me, would not be everlasting; whose prison, if he imprisoned me, would not hold me forever; who, if he sentenced me to death, would not sentence me to death eternal; and whom I could persuade with words and bribe with money, even so I would still cry.

"And now I am being led before the Sovereign of Sovereigns, the Holy One, who lives and endures forever. If God is angry with me, God's anger is everlasting. If God imprisons me, God's prison will hold me forever. If God sentences me to die, it is to death eternal. And I cannot persuade God with words or bribe God with money. And furthermore, there are two paths that lie before me. One path leads to Paradise and the other to Gehinnom, and I do not know on which path I will be taken. Should I not then weep?" (Talmud Berachot 28b).

5. The Martyrdom of Rabbi Hananiah ben Teradyon: The background for this story is the Hadrianic persecution follow-

ing the year 135 C.E. During the Roman occupation of Palestine, the leading rabbis of the country continued to meet with colleagues and teach Torah to their students, in defiance of the Roman government. Each was killed for the sanctification of God's name. As part of the penitential prayers of the Musaf additional service on Yom Kippur, the traditional prayer book includes a martyrology section that records the death of the ten rabbis killed by the Romans (including Rabbi Hananiah ben Teradyon), all for the sanctification of God's name.

Rabbi Hananiah ben Teradyon was found by the Romans studying the Torah, holding public gatherings of his students, and keeping a Torah scroll next to his heart. He did all of these things in violation of Roman law.

The Romans then wrapped him in the Torah scroll. Placing wood around him, they set everything on fire. The Romans then brought tufts of wool that had been soaked in water and placed them next to his heart so that he would die even more slowly.

His students called to him, "Rabbi, what do you see?"

Rabbi Hananiah answered, "The parchment is being burned but the letters of the Torah are soaring on high."

"Open your mouth so that the fire will penetrate you," they said.

And the rabbi answered, "Let God who gave me my soul take it away, but let no one injure himself" (Talmud Avodah Zarah 18a).

6. The Death of Rabban Gamaliel: This Talmudic story describes the origin of the custom of treating both rich and poor alike, with equal respect, according to matters of life and particularly death.

Formerly, they used to bring food to a house of mourning. Rich people were known to always bring baskets of gold and silver, and poor people brought baskets made of willow twigs. This made the poorer people feel ashamed. Then a law was passed that said everyone should use baskets of willow twigs, out of deference to the poor.

There was also a time when they used to serve drinks in a house of mourning. Rich people would serve their drinks in white glasses and the poor in less expensive colored ones. And once again, the poor felt ashamed. Then a law was passed that required everyone to serve their drinks in colored glasses, in deference to the poor.

Formerly they used to bring out the deceased for burial with the rich on a tall ornamented bed and the poor in a plain box. When the poor felt ashamed, they enacted a law that all should be brought out in a plain pine box, in deference to the poor.

And finally, the expense of burying the dead was even harder for a family to bear than death itself, so that some families tried to escape in order to rid themselves of the expense. This continued to occur until Rabban Gamliel ordered that he be buried in a plain linen shroud instead of in expensive garments. And since his time, Jewish people have been buried in plain white linen shrouds. (Talmud Moed Katan, 27–27b)

7. Rabbi Nachman's Death: While some may express their fear of death differently from others, few among us truly want to leave this earth. This Talmudic story reflects one particular rabbi's fear of dying.

While seated at the bedside of Rabbi Nachman, Rava watched him as he slipped into death.

Rabbi Nachman said to Rava, "Please tell the Angel of Death not to torture me."

Rava replied, "You are a man of great honor. You may speak directly to the angel."

Nachman answered, "Who is honored, who is distinguished, who is singled out before the Angel of Death?"

As Rabbi Nachman lay dying, Rava said, "Show yourself to me after you die."

Rabbi Nachman died and did appear to Rava in a dream. Rava asked, "Did you suffer much pain?"

Rabbi Nachman answered, "It was as easy as taking a hair from a pitcher of milk. But if God were not to say to me, 'Go back to the world as you were before,' I would not want to go. For the fear of death is very great there" (Talmud Moed Katan 28a).

8. The Death of Rabbi: In Jewish tradition, it is generally not acceptable to pray to hasten the death of another person. This Talmudic story describes an occasion where one prays for the death of a Talmudic sage who was suffering greatly.

On the day that Rabbi was dying, the rabbis proclaimed a public fast and offered prayers for God's divine mercy. They also decreed that whoever said Rabbi had died would be stabbed with a sword.

Rabbi's handmaid climbed to the roof and prayed, "The angels want Rabbi to join them, and the mortals want Rabbi to remain with them; may it be Your will, O God, that the mortals overpower the angels."

However, when the handmaid saw how much Rabbi was suffering, she again prayed, "May it be Your will that the angels overpower the mortals."

As the rabbis continued their prayers for mercy, the handmaid picked up a pitcher and threw it from the roof down to the ground. For a moment they stopped praying, and the soul of Rabbi departed. (Talmud Ketubot 104a)

9. The Death of Rabbi Meir's Children: This story from the Midrash is a tale about the two sons of Rabbi Meir who died on the Sabbath at home while their father was in the synagogue. Rabbi Meir's wise wife, Beruriah, one of the few women in the Talmud cited for her own wisdom, was home at the time. The rabbis relate this painful story because they are interested in determining how to handle such a difficult situation, especially since Jewish law expressly forbids mourning on the holy Sabbath. This tale is given as a commentary on Proverbs 31:10: "A woman of valor, who can find her?"

One Sabbath afternoon, when Rabbi Meir had returned to the synagogue to study, his two sons fell violently ill and died. Their mother, Beruriah, was overcome with grief. But what could she do? The Sabbath was a day of joy. All the laws of mourning are suspended on the Sabbath. She carried the two boys into her bedroom and covered them. In the evening, Rabbi Meir returned home from the House of Study. "Where are the children?" he asked. "I missed them at the synagogue."

Instead of answering the question, Beruriah handed him a cup of wine so that he could make Havdalah and usher out the Sabbath from their midst. After reciting the prayers of Havdalah, Rabbi Meir again asked his wife, "Where are the two boys?"

She replied, "Sometimes they go someplace, and now they're on their way." She then placed the evening meal before him and they both ate.

After reciting the blessing after the meal she said to him, "I would like to ask you a question."

He told her, "Ask your question."

She said, "A short time ago some precious jewels were entrusted to my care. I became so attached to them that I regarded them as if they were my own. Now, the true owner has come to take them back. Should we return them or not?"

He replied, "I am very surprised that you do not know the law and you would ask me such a question. Naturally, the jewels belong to the owner and must be returned."

She responded, "I would not have returned them without your consent." Beruriah then gently led her husband by the hand to the room and slowly lifted the sheet from the bodies of their dead sons.

He began to cry and shouted, "My sons, my sons."

Tearfully she reminded him, "Did you not say that we must return to the rightful Owner that which has been entrusted to us? Our sons were the jewels that God left with us." Together they wept, and they said, "God has given and God has now taken away. Blessed is the righteous Judge" (Proverbs Rabbah 31:10; Yalkut, Proverbs 964).

DEATH AND BURIAL OF FAMOUS BIBLICAL PERSONALITIES

1. Death of Absalom: This Biblical narrative reminds us that we ought not to become overly melancholy when death strikes. We should not grieve too much. Instead, what is important is the memory of those whom we love who have died and to continue living life in their memory—through the examples they have set before us.

It happened that the child did die. And the servants of King David were afraid to tell him that the child was dead, for they reasoned, "While his child was still alive, he did not listen to us when we spoke to him. How, then, can we now tell him that the child is dead? If we do, he may do himself harm."

When King David noticed that his servants were whispering to each other, he realized right then that the child was dead. Then King David asked his servants, "Is the child dead?" They answered, "He is dead."

King David arose from the ground and washed and changed his clothes, went to the House of God, and there he prayed. Then he went to his own home and they set food before him and he ate. His servants asked him, "What is this that you have done?" And King David replied, "While the child was still alive, I fasted and wept, for I said, 'Who knows whether God will be gracious to me, that the child may live?' But now he is dead, why should I not eat? Can I bring him back? I shall go to him, but he will not return to me" (II Samuel, chapter 12).

2. Death of Aaron: Preparation for death can be made by some for whom death is imminent. This story attempts to explain Aaron's preparation for death and the death itself.

When Aaron was approaching the time of his death, God said to his brother Moses, "Go to your brother and tell him about his impending death."

The next morning Moses arose and went to Aaron's tent. Aaron asked, "Why have you come to my tent so early in the morning?"

Moses replied, "I am worried about a certain section of the Torah that I was thinking about all night long, so I came to you."

Aaron then asked, "Where is the problem found?"

Moses answered, "I believe it is somewhere in the Book of Genesis."

They brought out the Torah scroll and began to read. At each part of the creation story, Moses said, "God made it beautiful." But when they reached the story of the creation of Adam, Moses said, "What can be said about Adam, who brought death to the world? Look, Aaron, I have prevailed over angels and you have stopped the plague of death, but even so our own end will be death. How many more years do you think we have?"

Aaron answered, "Very few."

Moses continued to get closer and closer to the subject of death until he referred to the surety of his own death. Soon Aaron began to feel that he would soon die and asked his brother Moses, "Did you come here to tell me about my own death?"

"Yes," answered Moses.

Soon thereafter Moses asked his brother, "Are you reconciled to the idea that you will die?"

Aaron responded, "Yes."

Then Moses said, "Let's together climb up to Mount Hor."

So Moses, Aaron and Aaron's son Eleazar went up the mountain as all the people watched, thinking that they had been called to receive God's instructions. Had they known the true purpose of the journey, they probably would have stopped them and begged mercy for Aaron.

Reaching the top of Mount Hor, they found a cave, and upon entering it they saw a lit lamp and a bed. Everything had been prepared by God. Moses was told to remove Aaron's priestly clothes. As he took off each garment, his son Eleazar put it on—just as darkness began to surround Aaron.

Then Moses spoke. "Aaron, when our sister Miriam died, you and I attended to her and buried her. At your death, you are attended to by Eleazar and me. But when I die, who will attend my burial?"

God then answered, "I promise that I will attend to you."

Moses then continued and said, "Brother Aaron, lie down on this couch and stretch out your hands. Close your eyes and your lips."

Aaron followed these instructions. Then God's Presence descended and touched Aaron and his soul left him. Moses and Eleazar kissed Aaron and the Cloud of Glory covered him.

God then told them, "Leave the cave."

Moses and Eleazar left, and the cave closed by itself.

When Moses and Eleazar descended Mount Hor, all the people stood and watched. They looked for Aaron, the lover of peace. When they finally realized that only two were coming down from the mountain, their concern was aggravated by Satan, who incited them against Moses and Eleazar. The community divided itself into three factions.

One faction said, "Moses killed Aaron out of jealousy."

A second cried out, "Eleazar killed his father out of his desire to succeed him."

The third faction suggested that Aaron died a natural death.

When Moses and Eleazar finally reached the people, the people demanded to know what happened to Aaron. Moses said to them, "God has taken him to the World to Come."

"We do not believe you," they retorted. "You must have had a disagreement and you killed Aaron for saying something you didn't like."

The people became wild with anger and were about to stone Moses and Eleazar when God ordered the angels to open the cave and bring out Aaron's coffin, which was seen by all of the people as it stood suspended in the heavens, surrounded by singing angels. So we read in the Bible, "And all the people saw that Aaron was dead" (Numbers 20:29). And what were the angels singing? "He entered into peace, they rest in their beds each one that walks in his uprightness" (Isaiah 57:2; Yalkut, Chukkat 764).

3. Jacob's Death: This rabbinic story attempts to explain the timing of the death of Jacob, who had gathered his sons together in order to receive his blessing, as reflected in Genesis 49:1–33.

Jacob called his sons and said to them, "Assemble yourselves and I will tell you." Jacob wanted to reveal the future to his children, but the Divine Spirit left him at that very moment. In truth, it was because it would be wrong for them to know what the future held. But Jacob said, "Perhaps one of my children will turn out to be no good. After all, Abraham had Ishmael, and Isaac had Esau."

Upon hearing these words, his children proclaimed, "Hear O Israel, Adonai our God, Adonai is One. Just as there is only one God for you, so for us there is only One God."

Reassured, Jacob then proclaimed, "Praised be God's Name forever and ever" (Talmud Pesachim 56a; Genesis Rabbah 98:4).

4. Death of Moses (1): One of the most puzzling aspects of Moses' leadership was his inability to enter the Promised Land. One wonders why God chose Moses to lead the people from slavery only to have him die in the wilderness just before crossing the Jordan River. This story attempts to explain theologically why God punished Moses and would not allow him to enter the Promised Land.

As Moses grew closer to his death, he began to pray to God for forgiveness for his sins. He wanted to be allowed to enter the Promised Land. Moses prayed, "O Sovereign of the Universe, You chose me in mercy to be Your servant. You have performed great miracles in Egypt. But now You say to me that I will die and my end will be like dust and worms."

God replied, "No person can escape death. Even Adam, who I made with My own hands, was doomed to die."

Moses responded, "O God, You gave only one command to the first person, and Adam disobeyed it."

God then responded, "I have heard enough. Speak to Me no longer."

But Moses continued to plead, "You forgive all Your creatures many sins with Your mercy and kindness. Cannot You overlook my one single sin?"

God answered, "I have made two vows. First, you will die before the Israelites enter the Promised Land. Second, Israel shall be forgiven and not be allowed to die. If I break My first vow, I must also cancel My second, and Israel will have to die."

To this Moses replied, "Rather shall I and a thousand like me die than a single soul in Israel" (Deuteronomy Rabbah 11:10).

5. Death of Moses (2): Since there is little biblical material that describes the death of Moses, much of what is written in the tradition concerning his death is taken from the Midrash. Even the burial place of Moses is shrouded in secrecy. This tale is taken from the Midrash on the Book of Proverbs (chapter 14). This legend takes advantage of the lack of knowledge about Moses' burial place by providing us with details that serve to describe our teacher in familiar human terms. We learn some interesting details about preparing for death both from the perspective of one who is dying and from those who survive Moses as future leaders of the Jewish community.

This account is based on Rabbi Simon's interpretation of the verse in Isaiah (58:8) "Your righteousness shall walk before you." Rabbi Simon says that this verse refers to the death of Moses, since it is written in the Book of Deuteronomy, "He comes as the head of the people, for he has performed the righteousness of God."

> Rabbi Abbahu said, "Come let us see how difficult it was at the hour of Moses', our master's, departure from the world. For when God told him, 'Moses, your time has come to leave the world,' Moses began to cry and scream. He asked God, 'Master of the Universe, was it for nothing that I spent all of my strength working for my people? Now shall my finale be the grave, my end as dust? If You could see it my way, You would cause me suffering but not hand me over to the pangs of death.' Of this David spoke, 'God, afflict me with suffering, but do not let me die' " (Psalm 118:18).
>
> "God answered Moses, 'Moses, I have taken an oath that one's leadership may not overlap another's by even a hairbreadth. Thus

far, you were leader of the Israelites; now it is time for Joshua to be their new leader.' "

"With this Moses answered God, 'Lord of the Universe, in the past I was the master and Joshua was my student. Now, I'll be his disciple and he shall be my master. Just don't let me die.' "

"God said, 'If you can do it, Moses, go right ahead.' "

"Moses immediately went to Joshua's door, where he stood in service upon Joshua with his arms crossed and body bowed. Joshua did not truly realize that it was Moses standing in service upon him."

"As was their custom, the Israelites rose early to pay their respects at Moses' door, but on this day they did not find him. They asked, 'Where can Moses be?' and they were told, 'He rose early in the morning to pay his respects at Joshua's door.' So they went and found Joshua seated and Moses standing as a servant before him. They asked, 'Joshua, Joshua, what is this you have done? Moses your master stands in service upon you?' "

"At that moment Joshua realized what was happening. Immediately he fell on his face before Moses and cried, 'Father, Master. You have raised me since I was a child, and you have taught me wisdom.' "

"The sons of Aaron stood on Moses' right and Joshua on his left. They asked him, 'Moses, what have you done?' He replied, 'Leave me alone, for God has told me that I should do this for Joshua so I will not die.' "

Rabbi Shmuel bar Nachmani quoted Rabbi Yochanan, "At that moment all of the Israelites sought to stone Joshua to death but for the pillar of cloud that interposed between them."

"They then said to Moses, 'Conclude the Torah for us.' But all of the traditions were forgotten by Moses and he did not know how to answer them."

"At this failure Moses fell to his face and said, 'O God, my death is better than my life' " (Jonah 4:3).

"When God saw that Moses was ready to die, God eulogized him, 'It is written, 'Who will stand up to Me for this nation of wicked, who will stand watch for Me on behalf of this nation of evildoers?' Who will stand up to Me in the wars of My children when they sin before Me?" (Psalm 94:16)

"At that moment the angel Michael came and bowed before God and said, 'Sovereign of the Universe, Moses was Yours in life, so he is Yours in death.' God responded, 'I lament not for Moses but for Israel, for many was the time that they sinned and he stood and prayed and tempered My anger, as it is said, 'God would have destroyed them but for Moses, God's chosen one, who stood in the breach and assuaged God's anger from its destroying fury" (Psalm 106:23).

"The Israelites then came and said to Moses, 'The moment for your departure from this world has arrived.' He said to them, 'Israel, O my children, forgive me for all that I have troubled you.' They answered, 'Our Master, Moses, you are forgiven.' They then said to him, 'Moses, forgive us all that we have angered you.' He told them, 'My children, you are forgiven, you are forgiven.' "

"They came and told him, 'But half a moment remains for you to depart this world.' He took his two hands and folded them upon his heart. Crying, he said, 'Surely my two hands, which received the Torah from the mouth of God, will now fall to the grave.' "

"They came and said to him, 'The moment for your departure from this world is ending.' At that moment Moses cried out mightily to God. He said, 'Master of both Worlds, if You take my soul in this world, will You return it to me in the Coming World?' "

"God answered, 'By your life. Just as you were the head of them all in this world, so will you be the head of them all in the Future World,' as it is written, "He comes as the head of the people" (Deuteronomy 33:21). Why so? Because of the righteousness he performed for Israel, as it is said, 'He has done the righteousness of God, and His judgment is with Israel' (Deuteronomy 33:21)".

Rabbi Nehemiah explained, "What did he do? He taught them Torah, laws and righteousness" (Proverbs Rabbah, chapter 14).

6. The Burial of Moses: This Talmudic story is a commentary on the verse from Deuteronomy 34:6 "And God buried him in a valley in the land of Moab, over against Beth Peor." It is an attempt to establish God's reason for not clearly identifying the place of Moses's burial.

The wicked rulers of Rome once ordered a military party at Beth Peor in an attempt to find the sepulcher of Moses. When they ascended on high ground, it appeared as if it were in the valley. However, when they stood in the valley, it appeared as if it were on high ground.

Rabbi Hama ben Haninah said, "Why was the burial place of Moses hidden from all people's knowledge? Because God knew that the time in the future would come when the Temple would be destroyed and Israel would be exiled from their land. If the Israelites knew where Moses was buried, they would be tempted to go to the sepulcher and cry and plead to Moses, saying, 'Moses, pray for us.' Moses would do so and the decree would be annulled, because the righteous are even more precious to God after their death than while they are alive" (Talmud Sotah 13a–b).

7. Death of David: If only we knew the day of our death, perhaps we could live in anticipation of it. Since we can never know when we will die, only that we will indeed die, the rabbis have taught us to repent on the day of our death and live each day as if it were our last. This Talmudic story focuses on King David's attempt to discover the day of his death.

King David said to the Holy Blessed One, "Master of the Universe, let me know when I will die." God said to David, "It is My own decree that no human beings will be told their day of death." So David asked, "Then what will be the measure of my days?" To this, God answered, "it is My own decree that no humans should be told the measure of their days." [David continued,] "Let me know when I will die." So God responded, "You will die on Shabbat." David pleaded, "Let me die on the first day of the week." But God responded, "On that day, your son Solomon's rule will begin. One's rule must not impinge on the other's rule, not even by a hair's breadth." God quoted the psalms [that are attributed to David]: " 'A day in Your courts is better than a thousand elsewhere' (84:11). It is better for Me that you sit and study Torah on one day than to receive a thousand burnt sacrifices that your son Solomon will offer up before Me on the altar."

From that point on, David sat and studied throughout the day every Shabbat. On the day on which he was about to die, the Angel of Death came to David, but the angel was unable to touch David because he never ceased studying. The angel thought to himself, "What shall I do to him?" David had a garden behind his home. The angel went to the garden and violently shook the trees. When David rose from his study in order to investigate the noise, as he went down the stairs, a step broke under his feet. He fell silent and his soul departed (Talmud Shabbat 30a–b).

8. Rekekah's Death and Rachel's Burial: The following Midrashic story explains both the reason why Rebekah's death is not recorded in the Bible and the reason why Rachel was buried on the road to Ephrat (and not in the cave of Machpelah).

When Rekekah died, it was asked: Who will walk before her casket? Abraham is dead. Isaac stays home because his eyes are dim, and Jacob has gone to Paddanaram. Should wicked Esau walk before her bier, people will say, "A curse on the breast that gave suck to such a one." What did they do? They took her out for burial at night. For that reason, Scripture does not record her death.

"And Rachel died, and was buried on the road to Ephrat" (Genesis 35:19). Why did Jacob see fit to bury Rachel on the road to Ephrat? Because our father Jacob foresaw that they who were to be exiled would pass by way of Ephrat. Therefore he buried her there, so that she might beseech mercy for them. Referring to this, Scripture says, "A voice is heard in Ramah, lamentation, and bitter weeping, Rachel weeping for her children" (Jeremiah 31:15; Genesis Rabbah 82:10).

9. Death of Sarah: The Bible does not mention the way in which Sarah died. We only know that her death is mentioned after the story of the binding of Isaac, and thus rabbinic theories abound connecting this event to her death. The following legend presents us with a description of Sarah's death.

Rabbi Zechariah said: The ram that had been created at the twilight of the sixth day of creation was running to and fro in its eagerness to be offered in place of Isaac, but Samael [Satan] kept blocking him in order to make Abraham's substitute offering impossible, with the result that both the ram's horns got entangled in the branches of a tree. What did that ram do then? It stretched out its foreleg to tap Abraham's cloak. Abraham looked behind him, saw the ram, extricated him, and brought him as an offering instead of his son.

At the time Isaac was bound, Satan went to Sarah, appearing to her in the form of Isaac. When Sarah saw him, she asked, "My son, what did your father do to you?" He replied, "My father took me, led me up hills and down into valleys, until finally he brought me up to the summit of a high and towering mountain, where he built an altar, set out the firewood, bound me upon the altar, and grasped a knife to cut my throat. Had not the Holy One said to him, 'Lay not your hand upon the boy,' I would have been slaughtered. Even before Satan finished his tale, Sarah's soul left her (Tanchuma Vayera, paragraph 23; Ecclesiastes Rabbah, 9:7).

SUICIDE: TAKING ONE'S OWN LIFE

1. The following Talmudic story describes various incidents to determine when a suicide is such that no death rites are to be performed.

For a suicide, no rites whatsoever should be observed. Rabbi Ishmael said: "He may be lamented: 'Alas, misguided fool. Alas, misguided fool.' "

Whereupon Rabbi Akiva said to him: "Leave him to his oblivion. Neither bless him nor curse him."

There may be no rending of clothes, no baring of shoulders, no eulogizing for him. But people should line up for him, and the mourner's blessing should be recited over him, out of respect for the living. The general rule is: The public should participate in whatsoever is done out of respect for the living; it should not participate in whatsoever is done out of respect for the dead.

Who is to be accounted a suicide? Not one who climbs to the top of a roof and falls to his death. Rather it is one who says, "Behold, I am going to climb to the top of the tree," or "to the top of the roof, and then throw myself down to my death," and thereupon others see him climb to the top of the tree or to the top of the roof and fall to his death. Such a one is presumed to be a suicide, and for such a person no rites whatsoever should be observed.

If a person is found strangled hanging from a tree, or slain impaled upon a sword, he is presumed to have taken his own life unwittingly; to such a person no rites whatsoever may be denied.

It happened that the son of Gorgos ran away from school. His father threatened to box his ears. In terror of his father, the boy went off and cast himself into a cistern. The incident was brought before Rabbi Tarfon, who ruled: "No rites whatsoever are to be denied him."

Another incident is that of a child from Bene Berak who broke a flask. His father threatened to box his ears. In terror of his father, the child went off and cast himself into a cistern. The matter was brought before Rabbi Akiva, who ruled: "No rites whatsoever are to be denied him."

As a result, the Sages said: "A man should not threaten his child. He should spank him at once, or else hold his peace and say nothing" (Talmud Semachot 2:1–5).

2. The following rabbinic deliberation tells on what occasion it might be permissible according to Jewish law to take one's own life.

It would seem that even if he was captured by Gentiles, and was afraid that they would torture him until he worshipped foreign god, still he should not kill himself, and should suffer the tortures according to his capacity. And he who comes to purify himself is helped from heaven.

However, if one is afraid that he will be tortured for the sake of other Jews, and God forbid, some Jews will be lost (as some false monarchs do), when they torture an individual Jew with reference to the general populace (apparently to get information), and one will thereby cause the death of many, one is permitted to kill himself, and perhaps Saul, of blessed memory, intended this when he fell on his sword, as he felt that if he feel alive into their hands they would violate him and torture him. And probably the children of Israel would not be able to see and listen to the difficulties of the king, and they would not prevent themselves from avenging him, and saving him, and consequently thousands of Israel would fail.

And possibly Saul's suicide was due to the fact that a king, who is the anointed of God, must not allow himself to die at the hands of Gentiles where death by torture and humiliation would, in the beliefs of our religion, bring about a desecration of God's name (S. Luria, *Yam Shel Sh'lomo* (Prague, 1715), Talmud Baba Kama, chapter. 8, no. 59).

3. **The following rabbinic tale, involving a suicide, tells of the origin of the law of what to do with one's tefillin when one needs to use the bathroom.**

It once happened that a certain student, upon entering the bathroom, left his tefillin in a hole adjoining the public way, and a harlot passed by and took them, and she came to the Bet HaMidrash and said, "See what so-and-so gave me for hire," and when the student heard it, he went to the top of the roof and threw himself down and killed himself. Thereupon they ordained that a man should hold the tefillin in his garment and in his hand and then go in (Talmud Berachot 23a).

4. **This rabbinic tale describes the suicide of young priests during the time of the destruction of the First Temple. They did not feel worthy of the task of acting as spiritual leaders on behalf of the people.**

Our rabbis have taught: When the First Temple was about to be destroyed, bands upon bands of young priests with the keys of the Temple in their hands assembled, mounted the roof of the Temple, and exclaimed: "Master of the Universe, as we did not have the merit to be faithful treasurers, these keys are handed back into Your keeping." They then threw the keys up toward heaven. And there emerged the figure of a hand which received the keys from them. Whereupon, they jumped and fell into the fire. It is an allusion to them that the prophet Isaiah laments: "The burden concerning the Valley of Vision. What ails you now, that you have all gone up to the housetops, you that are full of uproar, a tumultuous city, a joyous town. Your slain are not slain with the sword, nor dead in battle." Of the Holy Blessed One, it is said, "shouting and crying at the mount" (Talmud Taanit 29a).

TEN

WORDS OF COMFORT:
READINGS AND REFLECTIONS

Following are readings taken from traditional Jewish sources. Feel free to use them in any way that you see fit. They are intended to provide you with more insights into the nature of life and death. Hopefully you will find some of these thoughts of great comfort as well.

1. A person had three friends. One friend was loved most dearly. The second was also loved. But the third was regarded with the least affection. One day the elders commanded this person to appear before them immediately. The person was greatly alarmed. Had someone falsely accused him? In fear and trembling, the person called upon each of the friends.

First, the person turned to the dearest of friends, and was greatly disappointed when this friend found it impossible to go to the elders of the community.

Next, the person turned to his second friend: "Will you go with me?" But the latter answered: "I will go with you only as far as the city gates, but I cannot enter with you into the city."

In desperation, the person finally appealed to the third friend, the one to whom there was the least amount of devotion. Without hesitation, this neglected friend said: "Certainly I will accompany you, but first I'll go immediately to the City and plead for you with the elders.

The first friend is one's wealth which one must leave behind when departing from this world, as it is written: "Riches profit not on the day of reckoning."

The second friend is one's relatives, who can only follow a person to the graveside, as it is written: "No person can by any means redeem his fellow person from death."

The third least-considered friend, is the good deeds of the person's life. These can never go away and can even precede you to plead your cause before God, as it is written: "And your righteousness shall go before you" (Adapted from Pirke de Rabbi Eliezer).

2. Remember your Creator in the days of your youth
Before the evil days come and the years draw near,
Of which you will say, 'I have no pleasure in them.'
Before the sun grows dark,
And the light of the moon and the stars,
And the clouds return after the rain.
In the day when the watchmen of the house tremble,
And the strong men are bent.
The grinding maidens cease, for they are few,
And the ladies peering through the lattices grow dim.
When the doubled doors on the street are shut,
And the voice of the mill becomes low.
One wakes at the sound of a bird,
And all the daughters of song are laid low.
When one fears to climb a height,
And terrors lurk in a walk.

When the almond tree blossoms
The grasshopper becomes a burden,
And the caperberry can no longer stimulate desire.
So man goes to his home,
While the hired mourners walk about in the street.
Before the silver cord is severed,
And the golden bowl is shattered,
The pitcher is broken at the spring,
And the wheel is shattered at the pit.
The dust returns to the earth as it was,
And the spirit returns to God who gave it (Ecclesiastes 12:1–7).

3. Fear not the sentence of death
Remember them that have been before you, and those that come after;
This is the sentence from God over all flesh.
My son, according as you have, do well unto yourself,
And bring offering worthily to God.
Do well to your friend before you die,
And according to your ability, stretch out your hand and give to him.
Death is better than a bitter life,
And eternal rest than a continuous sickness;
Whoever fears God, it shall go well with him at the last
And in the day of his death he shall be blessed (Selections from Ben Sira).

4. The future is not like this world. In the future world there is no eating or drinking, no propagation or business or jealousy or hatred or competition, but the righteous sit with their crowns on their heads feasting on the brightness of the divine presence (Talmud Berachot 17a).

5. Rabbi Simeon the son of Elazar said: "Do not appease your fellow in the hour of his anger, and do not comfort him in the hour when his dead lies before him" (Pirke Avot, 4:23).

6. Rava said: "When a person is brought to judgment in the world to come, questions will be asked: Did you conduct your affairs with integrity? Did you set aside fixed times for the study of the Torah? Did you occupy yourself with the raising of a family? Did you hope for Israel's redemption and for universal peace? Did you search for wisdom? Did you acquire understanding? If the answer to these questions is 'yes,' but the person did not treasure reverence for God, all the learning and the fulfillment of the commandments are of little value" (Talmud Shabbat 31a).

7. These are the things the fruits of which a person enjoys in this world, while the stock remains for him for the world to come: honoring parents, the practice of deeds of kindness, timely attendance at the house of study mornings and evenings, hospitality to wayfarers, helping the needy bride, attending the dead to the grave, devotion in prayer and making peace between a man and his fellow. The study of Torah is basic to them all (Talmud Peah 1:1).

8. Our exit from the world, as compared to and contrasted with one's entry into it, is portrayed by Rabbi Levi thus: of two vessels sailing on the high seas, the ship which has come into port is in the eyes of the wise much more an object of joy than the ship about to leave the harbor. Even thus should we contemplate our departure from this world and without sorrow or fear, seeing that at death we have already entered the harbor—the haven or rest in the world to come (Exodus Rabbah 48:1).

9. There is a time for everything
A time for all things under the sun,

A time to be born, and a time to die,
A time to plant and a time to uproot,
A time to kill and a time to heal,
A time to break down and a time to build up
A time to cry and a time to laugh,
A time to mourn and a time to dance,
A time to scatter and a time to gather,
A time to embrace and a time to refrain from embraces
A time to seek and a time to lose
A time to keep and a time to cast away
A time to rend and a time to sew
A time to keep silent and a time to speak,
A time to love and a time to hate,
A time to war and a time for peace (Ecclesiastes 3:1–8).

10. O God, the soul which You gave me is pure; You did create and form it. You did breathe it into me. You preserved it within me, and You will take it from me, but will restore it to me in time to come. As long as this soul is within me, I acknowledge You, O God and God of my ancestors, Sovereign of all works. Blessed are You, O God, who restores the souls into lifeless bodies (Daily Prayerbook).

11. Rabbi Nechuniah ben HaKaneh was asked by his students: "By virtue of what have you reached such good old age?" He replied: "Never in my life have I sought respect through the degradation of my fellow, nor has the curse of my fellow gone up with me upon my bed, and I have been generous with my money . . . .

Rabbi Zera was asked by his students: "By virtue of what have you reached such good old age?" He replied: "Never in my life have I been harsh with my household, nor have I stepped in front of one greater than myself, nor have I meditated on the Torah in filthy alleys, nor have I gone four cubits without Torah and without tefillin, nor have I slept in the House of Study, either a long sleep or a short nap, nor have I rejoiced in the downfall of my fellow, nor have I called my fellow by his nickname" (Talmud Megillah 28a).

12. Resh Lakish said to him: "Say something with regard to the praise of the Holy Blessed One," He spoke and said: "The God who is great in the abundance of His greatness, mighty and strong in the multitude of awe inspiring deeds, who revives the dead with His word, does great things that are unsearchable and wondrous works without number. Blessed are You, God, who revives the dead."

He then said to him, "Rise and say something with regard to the mourners," He spoke and said, "Our brothers, who are worn out, who are crushed by their bereavement, set your heart to consider this. This it is that stands forever, it is a path from the six days of creation. Many have drunk, many will drink, as the drinking of the first ones, so will be that of the last ones. Our brothers, the God of consolation, comfort you. Blessed be the One who comforts the mourners (Talmud Ketubot 8b).

13. A king once owned a large, beautiful, pure diamond of which he was justly proud, for it had not equal anywhere. One day, this diamond accidentally sustained a deep scratch. The king called in the most expert diamond cutters and offered them a great reward if they could remove the imperfection from this jewel. But none could repair the blemish. The king was sorely distressed.

After some time, a gifted craftsman came to the king and promised to make the rare diamond even more beautiful than it had been before the mishap. The king was impressed by his confidence and entrusted the precious stone to his care.

And the man kept his word. With superb artistry he engraved

a lovely rosebud around the imperfection, using the scratch to make the stem (Dubner Maggid, M'shalim).

14. I will lift up my eyes to the mountains. What is the source of my help? The source of my help is Adonai, Creator of Heaven and earth. Adonai will not let you falter; your Guardian will not slumber. Surely the Guardian of Israel will neither slumber nor sleep. Adonai is your protector, Adonai is your shelter at your right hand. The sun will not smite you by day, nor the moon by night. Adonai will guard you from all harm; God will preserve your soul. Adonai will guard your going and your coming, now and forever more (Psalm 121).

15. A rabbi was once passing through a field where he saw a very old man planting an oak tree. "Why are you planting the oak tree?" he asked. "Surely you do not expect to live long enough to see the acorn grow into a tree?"

The old man replied: "My ancestors planted trees not for themselves, but for us, in order that we might enjoy their shade or their fruit. I am doing likewise for all of those who come after me" (Talmud Taanit 23a).

16. Those who sow in tears shall reap with songs of joy (Psalm 126:5).

17. Adonai is my shepherd, I shall not want
Giving me repose in green meadows,
Leading me beside the still waters to restore my spirit.
Guiding me on the right path, for that is God's essence.
Though I walk through a valley of the shadow of death,
I fear no harm, for You are with me.
Your staff and Your rod comfort me.
You prepare a banquet for me in the presence of my foes.
You anoint my head with oil; my cup overflows.

Surely goodness and mercy shall follow me all the days of my life
And I shall dwell in the House of Adonai, forever (Psalm 23).

18. There are stars whose light reaches the earth only after they themselves have disintegrated and are no more. And there are people whose scintillating memory lights the world after they have passed from it. These lights which shine in the darkest night are those which illumine for us the path ... (Hannah Senesh).

19. I have set God always before me;
Surely God is at my right hand, I shall not be moved.
Therefore my heart is glad, and my glory rejoices;
May flesh also dwells in safety;
For your will not abandon my soul to the nether world;
Neither will You suffer Your godly one to see the pit.
You make me to know the path of life;
In Your presence is fullness of joy,
At Your right hand bless forever more (Selected verses from Psalm 16).

20. The souls of the righteous are in the hand of God,
And no torment shall touch them.
In the eyes of the foolish they seemed to have died;
And their departure has accounted to be to their hurt,
And their journeying away from us to be their ruin.
But they are in peace.
For even if in the sight of men they be punished,
Their hope is full of immortality.
And having borne a little chastening, they shall receive great good;
Because God made trial of them and found them worthy of Himself
(Wisdom of Solomon III: 1–6).

21. Rabbi Tarfon said: The day is short, and the work is great, and the laborers are sluggish, and the reward is much, and the Master

is urgent. He used to say, It is not your duty to complete the work, but neither are you free to desist from it. If you have studied much Torah, much reward will be given to you; and faithful is your Employer to pay you the reward of your labor; and know that the grant of reward unto the righteous will be in the time to come (Pirke Avot 2:20–21).

22. Rabbi Jacob said: This world is like a vestibule before the world to come. Prepare yourself in the vestibule, that you may enter into the hall. He used to say, "Better is one hour of repentance and good deeds in this world than the whole life of the world to come, and better is one hour of blissfulness of spirit in the world to come than the whole life of this world" (Pirke Avot 4:21).

23. Rabbi Yose, the son of Kisma, said, I was once walking by the way, when a man met me and greeted me, and I returned his greeting. He said to me, Rabbi, from what place are you? I answered: I come from a great city of sages and scribes. He said to me: If you are willing to dwell with us in our place, I will give you a thousand golden dinars and precious stones and pearls. I said to him, Were you to give me all the silver and gold, and precious stones and pearls in the world, I would not dwell anywhere but in a home of the Torah. Thus it is written in the Book of Psalms by the hands of King David of Israel, The law of your mouth is better to me than thousands of gold and silver. And not only so, but in the hour of a man's departure, neither silver nor gold nor precious stones nor pearls accompany him, but only Torah and good works, as it is said, When you walk it shall lead you; when you lie down it shall watch over you; and when you awaken it shall talk with you. When you walk it shall lead you—in this world. When you lie down it shall watch over you—in the grave. And when you awaken it shall talk with you—in the world to come. And it says,

The silver is mine, and the gold is mine, says Adonai Tzeva'ot (Pirke Avot 6:9).

24. Rabbi Meir said: When do we learn that as you should say a blessing over the good, so you should say a blessing over the evil? Because it says, 'Which Adonai your God gives you (Deuteronomy 8:10) And 'your God' means 'your judge'; in every judgement with which God judges you, whether the attribute of good or with the attribute of punishment, bless God (Talmud Berachot 48b).

25. When Rabbi Yochanan finished the Book of Job, he used to say the following: The end of man is to die, and the end of beast is to be slaughtered, and all are doomed to die. Happy is he who was brought up in the Torah and in whose labor was in the Torah and who has given pleasure to his Creator and who grew up with a good name and departed the world with a good name; and of him Solomon said: A good name is better than precious oil, and the day of death than the day of one's birth (Ecclesiastes 8:1; Talmud Berachot 17a).

26. It once came to pass that Hillel the elder was coming from a journey, and he heard a great cry in the city, and he said: I am confident that this does not come from my house. Of him Scripture says: He shall not be afraid of the evil tidings; his heart is steadfast trusting God (Psalm 112:7; Talmud Berachot 60a).

27. Rabbi Simeon ben Pazzi said in the name of Rabbi Joshua ben Levi in Bar Kappara's name: if one sheds tears for a worthy man, the Holy Blessed one counts them and lays them up in His treasure house, for it is said: You count my grievings: Put my tears into your bottle. Are they not in your book? (Psalm 66:9; Talmud Shabbat 105b)

28. "Blessed shall you be when you come in, and blessed shall you be when you go out" (Deuteronomy 28:3)—that your exit from the world shall be as your entry therein: just as you enter it without sin, so may you leave it without (Talmud Baba Metzia 107a).

29. Rabbi Simlai said: Six hundred and thirteen commandments were given to Moses, 365 negative commandments, answering to the number of the days of the year, and 248 positive commandments, answering to the number of the members of man's body. Then David came and reduced them to eleven (eleven commands are found in Psalm 15). Then came Isaiah, and reduced them to six. Then came Micah, and reduced them to three (as is seen in the great saying of Micah 6:80). Then Isaiah came again, and reduced them to two, as it is said, 'keep justice and do righteousness'. Then came Amos, and reduced them to one, as it is said, 'Seek me and live'. Or one may say, then came Habakkuk (2:4) and reduced them to one, as it is said, 'The righteous shall live by his faith' (Talmud Makkot 23b–24a).

30. A king had a vineyard in which he employed many workers, one of whom demonstrated special aptitude and skill. What did the king do? He took this laborer from his work and strolled through the garden conversing with him. When the workers came for their wages in the evening, the skilful worker also appeared among them and he received a full day's wages from the king. The other workers were angry at this and protested. 'We had labored the whole day while this man has worked but two hours; why does the king give him the full wage, even as to us?' The king said to them: 'Why are you angry? Through his skill he has done in two hours more than you have done all day.' So it is with Rabbi Abin ben Hiyya. In the twenty eight years of his life he has attained more in Torah than others in a hundred years (Jerusalem Talmud, Berachot 2:8; Ecclesiastes Rabbah 6).

31. A man has three friends: His children and household, his wealth and his good deeds. When about to depart form this world, he appeals to his children: 'Save me.' They say to him: 'there is no man that has power over the day of death' (Ecclesiastes 8:8); 'No man can by any means redeem his brother' (Psalm 49:8). His wealth replies to him: 'Riches profit not in the day of wrath' (proverbs 11:4) But his good deeds say to him: 'Before you come for judgment, we shall be there ahead of you' as it is written (Isaiah 58:8): 'And your righteousness shall go before you, the glory of God shall be your reward' (Pirke de Rabbi Eliezer, 34).

32. With regard to the great bliss which the soul is to attain in the future world, there is no possibility of comprehending or knowing it while we are in this world; seeing that here beneath we are sensible of that only which is good for the body. But with respect to the celestial bliss, it is so exceedingly great, that all earthy good can bear no comparison with it, except by way of figure. So that truly to estimate the happiness of the body in this world, as for instance in eating or drinking, is utterly impossible. That is what David meant in exclaiming, 'Oh, how abundant is Your goodness, which You have laid up for them that fear you' (Psalm 31:20; Mishnah Torah, Book of Knowledge, Laws of Repentance, 8:6).

Mourner's Kaddish

יִתְגַּדַּל וְיִתְקַדַּשׁ שְׁמֵהּ רַבָּא בְּעָלְמָה דִּי־בְרָא כִרְעוּתֵהּ,

וְיַמְלִיךְ מַלְכוּתֵהּ בְּחַיֵּיכוֹן וּבְיוֹמֵיכוֹן וּבְחַיֵּי דְכָל־בֵּית

יִשְׂרָאֵל, בַּעֲגָלָא וּבִזְמַן קָרִיב, וְאִמְרוּ: אָמֵן.

יְהֵי שְׁמֵי רַבָּא מְבָרַךְ לְעָלַם וּלְעָלְמֵי עָלְמַיָּא.

יִתְבָּרַךְ וְיִשְׁתַּבַּח, וְיִתְפָּאַר וְיִתְרוֹמַם וְיִתְנַשֵּׂא, וְיִתְהַדָּר

וְיִתְעַלֶּה וְיִתְהַלָּל שְׁמֵהּ דְּקוּדְשָׁא, בְּרִיךְ הוּא, לְעֵלָּא מִן־כָּל־

בִּרְכָתָא וְשִׁירָתָא, תֻּשְׁבְּחָתָא וְנֶחֱמָתָא דַּאֲמִירָן בְּעָלְמָא,

וְאִמְרוּ: אָמֵן.

יְהֵא שְׁלָמָא רַבָּא מִן־שְׁמַיָּא וְחַיִּים עָלֵינוּ וְעַל־כָּל־יִשְׂרָאֵל,

וְאִמְרוּ: אָמֵן.

עֹשֶׂה שָׁלוֹם בִּמְרוֹמָיו, הוּא יַעֲשֶׂה שָׁלוֹם עָלֵינוּ וְעַל־כָּל־

יִשְׂרָאֵל וְאִמְרוּ: אָמֵן.

Yit-ga-dal, ve-yit-ka-dash she-mei ra-ba be-al-ma di-ve-ra chi-re-u-tei,

ve-yam-lich mal-chu-tei be-cha-yei-chon u-ve-yo-mei-chon u-ve-cha-yei de-chol beit

Yis-ra-eil, ba-a-ga-la u-vi-ze-man ka-riv, ve-i-me-ru: a-mein.

Ye-hei she-mei ra-ba me-va-rach le-a-lam u-le-mei al-ma-ya.

Yit-ba-rach ve-yish-ta-bach, ve-yit-pa-ar ve-yit-ro-mam ve-yit-na-sei, ve-yit-ha-dar

ve-yit-a-leh ve-yit-ha-lal she-mei de-ku-de-sha, be-rich hu, le-ei-la min kol
bi-re-cha-ta ve-shi-ra-ta, tush-be-cha-ta ve-ne-che-ma-ta, da-a mi-ran be-
al-ma,

ve-i-me-ru; a-mein.

Ye-hei she-la-ma ra-ba min she-me-ya ve-cha-yim a-lei-nu ve-al kol
Yis-ra-eil,

ve-i-me-ru: a-mein.

O-seh sha-lom bi-me-ro-mav, hu ya-a-seh sha-lom a-lei-nu ve-al kol

Yis-ra-eil, ve-i-me-ru: a-mein.

Let the glory of God be extolled, let God's great name be hallowed, in the world whose creation God willed. May God's sovereignty soon prevail, in our own day, our own lives, and the life of
all Israel, and let us say Amen.

Let God's great name be blessed for ever and ever.

Let the name of God be glorified, exalted, and honored, though
God is beyond all the praises, songs, and adorations that we can
utter, and let us say Amen.

For us and for all Israel, may the blessing of peace and the
promise of life come true, and let us say Amen.

May God who causes peace to reign in the high heavens, let peace
descend on us, on all Israel and all the world, and let us say: Amen.

Prayers When Visiting a Cemetery

תהלים כ"ג

מִזְמוֹר לְדָוִד יְהוָֹה רֹעִי לֹא אֶחְסָר: בִּנְאוֹת דֶּשֶׁא יַרְבִּיצֵנִי עַל־מֵי מְנֻחוֹת
יְנַהֲלֵנִי: נַפְשִׁי יְשׁוֹבֵב יַנְחֵנִי בְמַעְגְּלֵי־צֶדֶק לְמַעַן שְׁמוֹ: גַּם כִּי־אֵלֵךְ בְּגֵיא
צַלְמָוֶת לֹא־אִירָא רָע כִּי־אַתָּה עִמָּדִי שִׁבְטְךָ וּמִשְׁעַנְתֶּךָ הֵמָּה יְנַחֲמֻנִי: תַּעֲרֹךְ
לְפָנַי שֻׁלְחָן נֶגֶד צֹרְרָי דִּשַּׁנְתָּ בַשֶּׁמֶן רֹאשִׁי כּוֹסִי רְוָיָה: אַךְ טוֹב וָחֶסֶד יִרְדְּפוּנִי
כָּל־יְמֵי חַיָּי וְשַׁבְתִּי בְּבֵית־יְהוָֹה לְאֹרֶךְ יָמִים:

PSALM 23: THE LORD IS MY SHEPHERD

The Lord is my shepherd, I shall not want. He makes me lie down
in green pastures. He leads me beside the still waters. He restores
my soul. He guides me in straight paths for His name's sake. Though
I walk in the valley of the shadow of death, I fear no evil, for You
are with me. Your staff and Your rod comfort me. You prepare a
banquet for me in the presence of my enemies. You annoint my
head with oil; my cup runs over. Surely goodness and mercy shall
follow me all the days of your life. And I shall dwell in the house
of God forever.

IN MEMORY OF A LOVED ONE

I lovingly recall _____; may he/she rest in peace. I
thank God for the gift of his/her life, for the pleasant memories
which are left behind. May the goodness and love with which he/
she touched my life continue to influence my life as I share these
qualities of kindness with others. May his/her soul be bound up in
the bond of life and endure as a source of blessing to all who
knew and loved him/her. Amen.

A WOMAN OF VALOR
(PROVERBS 31)

Eishet, hayil mi yimtza
v'rahok mip'ninim mikharah.
Batah bah lev ba'lah
v'shalal lo yehsar.
G'malat'hu tov v'lo ra
kol y'mei hayeha.
Darsha tzemer u-fishtim
vata'as b'hefetz kape'ha.
Hay'ta ko'oniyot soher
mimerhak tavi lahmah.
Vatakom b'od lailah
vatiten teref l'veita
v'hok l'na'aroteha.

A good wife, who can find?
She is more precious than rubies.
The heart of her husband trusts in her
And he has no lack of gain.
She does him good and not harm
All the days of her life.
She seeks wool and flax,
And works willingly with her hands.
She is like the merchant ships
She brings her food from afar.
She rises also while it is yet night,
And gives food to her household,
And a portion to her maidens:

PSALM 112: BLESSED IS THE MAN

Hal'luyah.
Ashrei ish yarei et Adonai
b'mitzvotav hafetz m'od.
Gibor ba'aretz yiyeh zaro
dor y'sharim y'vorakh.
Hon va'osher b'veito
v'tzid'kato omedet la'ad,
Zarah ba'hoshekh or
la-y'sharim.

Halleluya! Happy is the man who reveres Adonai,
Who greatly delights in God's commandments.
His descendents will be honored in the land,
The generation of the upright will be praised.
His household prospers and his righteousness lasts forever.
Light shines in the darkness for the upright.

EIL MALEI RACHAMIM

For male

אֵל מָלֵא רַחֲמִים, שׁוֹכֵן בַּמְּרוֹמִים, הַמְצֵא מְנוּחָה נְכוֹנָה תַּחַת כַּנְפֵי הַשְּׁכִינָה,
בְּמַעֲלוֹת קְדוֹשִׁים וּטְהוֹרִים כְּזֹהַר הָרָקִיעַ מַזְהִירִים, אֶת־נִשְׁמַת
בֶּן ⸺ שֶׁהָלַךְ לְעוֹלָמוֹ, בְּגַן
עֵדֶן תְּהֵא מְנוּחָתוֹ. אָנָּא, בַּעַל הָרַחֲמִים הַסְתִּירֵהוּ בְּסֵתֶר כְּנָפֶיךָ לְעוֹלָמִים,
וּצְרוֹר בִּצְרוֹר הַחַיִּים אֶת־נִשְׁמָתוֹ, יְיָ הוּא נַחֲלָתוֹ, וְיָנוּחַ בְּשָׁלוֹם עַל מִשְׁכָּבוֹ,
וְנֹאמַר אָמֵן.

*Eil malei rachamim sho-khein bam'romim, hamm-tzei, m'nukhah
n'khonah tahat kanfei ha-sh'khinah, b'ma-alot k'doshim u-t'horim
k'zohar ha-rakiya maz-hirim et nishmat ⸺ ben
⸺ she-halakh l'olamo, b'gan eiden t'hei m'nuhato. Ana,
ba-al ha-rahamim, hassti-rei-hu'b'seiter k'nafekha l'olamim, u-tzror bitzror ha-hayim et nishmato, Adonai hu nahalato, v'yanu-ah b'shalom
al mishkavo, v'nomar amen.*

God of compassion, grant perfect peace in Your sheltering Presence, among the holy and the pure who shine in the brightness of
the firmament, to the soul of our dear ⸺ who has
gone to his eternal rest. God of compassion, remember all his worthy deeds in the land of the living. May his soul be bound up in
the bond of everlasting life. May God be his inheritance. May he
rest in peace. And let us answer: Amen.

For female

אֵל מָלֵא רַחֲמִים, שׁוֹכֵן בַּמְּרוֹמִים, הַמְצֵא מְנוּחָה נְכוֹנָה תַּחַת כַּנְפֵי הַשְּׁכִינָה,
בְּמַעֲלוֹת קְדוֹשִׁים וּטְהוֹרִים כְּזֹהַר הָרָקִיעַ מַזְהִירִים אֶת־נִשְׁמַת
בַּת _____ שֶׁהָלְכָה לְעוֹלָמָהּ, _____
בְּגַן עֵדֶן תְּהֵא מְנוּחָתָהּ. אָנָּא, בַּעַל הָרַחֲמִים הַסְתִּירֶהָ בְּסֵתֶר כְּנָפֶיךָ לְעוֹלָמִים,
וּצְרוֹר בִּצְרוֹר הַחַיִּים אֶת־נִשְׁמָתָהּ, יְיָ הוּא נַחֲלָתָהּ, וְתָנִיחַ בְּשָׁלוֹם עַל
מִשְׁכָּבָהּ, וְנֹאמַר אָמֵן.

Eil malei rachamim sho-khein bam'romim, hamm-tzei m'nukhah
n'khonah tahat kanfei ha-sh'khinah, b'ma-alot k'doshim u't'horim
k'zohar ha'rakiya maz-hirim et nishmat _____ bat
_____ sheh-halkhah l'olamah, b'gan eiden t'hei m'nuhatah.
Ana, ba-al harahamim, hassti-reha b'seiter k'nafekha l'olamim, u-tzror
bitzror ha-hayim et nishmatah, Adonai hu nahalatah, v'tanu-ah
b'shalom al mishkavah, v'nomar amen.

God of compassion, grant perfect peace in Your sheltering Presence, among the holy and the pure who shine in the brightness of
the firmament, to the soul of our dear _____ who has
gone to her eternal rest. God of compassion, remember all her worthy
deeds in the land of the living. May her soul be bound up in the
bond of everlasting life. May God be her inheritance. May she rest
in peace. And let us answer: Amen.

MOURNER'S KADDISH

יִתְגַּדַּל וְיִתְקַדַּשׁ שְׁמֵהּ רַבָּא בְּעָלְמָא דִּי־בְרָא כִרְעוּתֵהּ,

וְיַמְלִיךְ מַלְכוּתֵהּ בְּחַיֵּיכוֹן וּבְיוֹמֵיכוֹן וּבְחַיֵּי דְכָל־בֵּית

יִשְׂרָאֵל, בַּעֲגָלָא וּבִזְמַן קָרִיב, וְאִמְרוּ: אָמֵן.

יְהֵי שְׁמֵי רַבָּא מְבָרַךְ לְעָלַם וּלְעָלְמֵי עָלְמַיָּא.

יִתְבָּרַךְ וְיִשְׁתַּבַּח, וְיִתְפָּאַר וְיִתְרוֹמַם וְיִתְנַשֵּׂא, וְיִתְהַדָּר

וְיִתְעַלֶּה וְיִתְהַלָּל שְׁמֵהּ דְּקוּדְשָׁא, בְּרִיךְ הוּא, לְעֵלָּא מִן־כָּל־

בִּרְכָתָא וְשִׁירָתָא, תֻּשְׁבְּחָתָא וְנֶחֱמָתָא דַּאֲמִירָן בְּעָלְמָא,

וְאִמְרוּ: אָמֵן.

יְהֵא שְׁלָמָא רַבָּא מִן־שְׁמַיָּא וְחַיִּים עָלֵינוּ וְעַל־כָּל־יִשְׂרָאֵל,

וְאִמְרוּ: אָמֵן.

עֹשֶׂה שָׁלוֹם בִּמְרוֹמָיו, הוּא יַעֲשֶׂה שָׁלוֹם עָלֵינוּ וְעַל־כָּל־

יִשְׂרָאֵל וְאִמְרוּ: אָמֵן.

Yit-ga-dal, ve-yit-ka-dash she-mei ra-ba be-al-ma di-ve-ra chi-re-u-tei,

ve-yam-lich mal-chu-tei be-cha-yei-chon u-ve-yo-mei-chon u-ve-cha-
yei de-chol beit

Yis-ra-eil, ba-a-ga-la u-vi-ze-man ka-riv, ve-i-me-ru: a-mein.

Ye-hei she-mei ra-ba me-va-rach le-a-lam u-le-mei al-ma-ya.

Yit-ba-rach ve-yish-ta-bach, ve-yit-pa-ar ve-yit-ro-mam ve-yit-na-sei, ve-
    yit-ha-dar
ve-yit-a-leh ve-yit-ha-lal she-mei de-ku-de-sha, be-rich hu, le-ei-la min kol
bi-re-cha-ta ve-shi-ra-ta, tush-be-cha-ta ve-ne-che-ma-ta, da-a mi-ran be-
    al-ma,
ve-i-me-ru; a-mein.
Ye-hei she-la-ma ra-ba min she-me-ya ve-cha-yim a-lei-nu ve-al kol
    Yis-ra-eil,
ve-i-me-ru: a-mein.

O-seh sha-lom bi-me-ro-mav, hu ya-a-seh sha-lom a-lei-nu ve-al kol

Yis-ra-eil, ve-i-me-ru: a-mein.

Let the glory of God be extolled, let God's great name be hallowed, in the world whose creation God willed. May God's sovereignty soon prevail, in our own day, our own lives, and the life of
all Israel, and let us say Amen.

Let God's great name be blessed for ever and ever.

Let the name of God be glorified, exalted, and honored, though
God is beyond all the praises, songs, and adorations that we can
utter, and let us say Amen.

For us and for all Israel, may the blessing of peace and the
promise of life come true, and let us say Amen.

May God who causes peace to reign in the high heavens, let peace
descend on us, on all Israel and all the world, and let us say: Amen.

THE BURIAL KADDISH

Mourners and those observing Yahrzeit:

יִתְגַּדַּל וְיִתְקַדַּשׁ שְׁמֵהּ רַבָּא בְּעָלְמָא דִּי בְרָא כִרְעוּתֵהּ, וְיַמְלִיךְ מַלְכוּתֵהּ בְּחַיֵּיכוֹן וּבְיוֹמֵיכוֹן וּבְחַיֵּי דְכָל־בֵּית יִשְׂרָאֵל, בַּעֲגָלָא וּבִזְמַן קָרִיב, וְאִמְרוּ אָמֵן.

Congregation and mourner:

יְהֵא שְׁמֵהּ רַבָּא מְבָרַךְ לְעָלַם וּלְעָלְמֵי עָלְמַיָּא.

Mourner:

יִתְבָּרַךְ וְיִשְׁתַּבַּח וְיִתְפָּאַר וְיִתְרוֹמַם וְיִתְנַשֵּׂא, וְיִתְהַדָּר וְיִתְעַלֶּה וְיִתְהַלָּל שְׁמֵהּ דְּקֻדְשָׁא, בְּרִיךְ הוּא לְעֵלָּא (לְעֵלָּא מִכָּל־) מִן כָּל־בִּרְכָתָא וְשִׁירָתָא, תֻּשְׁבְּחָתָא וְנֶחֱמָתָא דַּאֲמִירָן בְּעָלְמָא, וְאִמְרוּ אָמֵן.

יְהֵא שְׁלָמָא רַבָּא מִן שְׁמַיָּא וְחַיִּים עָלֵינוּ וְעַל כָּל־יִשְׂרָאֵל, וְאִמְרוּ אָמֵן.

עוֹשֶׂה שָׁלוֹם בִּמְרוֹמָיו, הוּא יַעֲשֶׂה שָׁלוֹם עָלֵינוּ וְעַל כָּל־יִשְׂרָאֵל, וְאִמְרוּ אָמֵן.

יהוה רֹעִי, לֹא אֶחְסָר.

The Lord is my shepherd, I shall not want.

בִּנְאוֹת דֶּשֶׁא יַרְבִּיצֵנִי,

He gives me repose in green meadows.

עַל מֵי מְנֻחוֹת יְנַהֲלֵנִי. נַפְשִׁי יְשׁוֹבֵב,

He leads me beside the still waters to revive my spirit.

יַנְחֵנִי בְמַעְגְּלֵי־צֶדֶק לְמַעַן שְׁמוֹ.

He guides me on the right path, for that is His nature.

גַּם כִּי אֵלֵךְ בְּגֵיא צַלְמָוֶת
לֹא אִירָא רָע כִּי אַתָּה עִמָּדִי.

Though I walk in the valley of the shadow of death,
I fear no harm, for You are with me.

שִׁבְטְךָ וּמִשְׁעַנְתֶּךָ הֵמָּה יְנַחֲמֻנִי.

Your staff and Your rod comfort me.

תַּעֲרֹךְ לְפָנַי שֻׁלְחָן נֶגֶד צֹרְרָי,

You prepare a banquet for me in the presence of my foes.

דִּשַּׁנְתָּ בַשֶּׁמֶן רֹאשִׁי, כּוֹסִי רְוָיָה.

You anoint my head with oil; my cup overflows.

אַךְ טוֹב וָחֶסֶד יִרְדְּפוּנִי כָּל־יְמֵי חַיָּי,

Surely goodness and kindness shall be my portion
all the days of my life.

וְשַׁבְתִּי בְּבֵית יהוה לְאֹרֶךְ יָמִים.

And I shall dwell in the House of the Lord forever.

PSALM 23

Mourners—May His great name be magnified and sanctified in
the world that is to be created anew, where He will revive the
dead, and raise them up into life eternal; will rebuild the city of
Jerusalem, and establish His temple in the midst thereof; and will
uproot all alien worship from the earth and restore the worship of
the true God. O may the Holy One, blessed be He, reign in His

sovereignty and glory during your life and during your days, and during the life of all the house of Israel, even speedily and at a near time, and say ye, Amen.

Congregation and Mourners—Let His great name be blessed for ever and to all eternity.

Mourners—Blessed, praised and glorified, exalted, extolled and honored, magnified and lauded be the name of the Holy One, blessed be He; though He be high above all blessings and hymns, praises and consolations, which are uttered in the world; and say ye; Amen.

Mourners—May there be abundant peace from heaven; and life for us and for all Israel; and say ye, Amen.

Mourners—He who maketh peace in His high places, may He make peace for us and for all Israel; and say ye, Amen.

YIZKOR REMEMBRANCE PRAYERS

In memory of a mother:

יִזְכֹּר אֱלֹהִים נִשְׁמַת אִמִּי מוֹרָתִי שֶׁהָלְכָה לְעוֹלָמָהּ. הִנְנִי נוֹדֵר
(נוֹדֶרֶת) צְדָקָה בְּעַד הַזְכָּרַת נִשְׁמָתָהּ. אָנָּא תְּהִי נַפְשָׁהּ צְרוּרָה
בִּצְרוֹר הַחַיִּים וּתְהִי מְנוּחָתָהּ כָּבוֹד, שְׂבַע שְׂמָחוֹת אֶת־פָּנֶיךָ,
נְעִימוֹת בִּימִינְךָ נֶצַח. אָמֵן.

May God remember the soul of my mother who has gone to her eternal home. In loving testimony to her life I pledge charity to help perpetuate ideals important to her. Through such deeds, and through prayer and memory, is her soul bound up in the bond of life. May I prove myself worthy of the gift of life and the many other gifts with which she blessed me. May these moments of meditation strengthen the ties that link me to her memory and to our entire family. May she rest forever in dignity and peace. Amen.

In memory of a father:

יִזְכֹּר אֱלֹהִים נִשְׁמַת אָבִי מוֹרִי שֶׁהָלַךְ לְעוֹלָמוֹ. הִנְנִי נוֹדֵר
(נוֹדֶרֶת) צְדָקָה בְּעַד הַזְכָּרַת נִשְׁמָתוֹ. אָנָּא תְּהִי נַפְשׁוֹ צְרוּרָה
בִּצְרוֹר הַחַיִּים וּתְהִי מְנוּחָתוֹ כָּבוֹד, שְׂבַע שְׂמָחוֹת אֶת־פָּנֶיךָ,
נְעִימוֹת בִּימִינְךָ נֶצַח. אָמֵן.

May God remember the soul of my father who has gone to his
eternal home. In loving testimony to his life I pledge charity to
help perpetuate ideals important to him. Through such deeds, and
through prayer and memory, is his soul bound up in the bond of
life. May I prove myself worthy of the gift of life and the many
other gifts with which he blessed me. May these moments of meditation strengthen the ties that link me to his memory and to our
entire family. May he rest forever in dignity and peace. Amen.

In memory of a husband:

יִזְכֹּר אֱלֹהִים נִשְׁמַת בַּעֲלִי שֶׁהָלַךְ לְעוֹלָמוֹ. הִנְנִי נוֹדֶרֶת צְדָקָה
בְּעַד הַזְכָּרַת נִשְׁמָתוֹ. אָנָּא תְּהִי נַפְשׁוֹ צְרוּרָה בִּצְרוֹר הַחַיִּים
וּתְהִי מְנוּחָתוֹ כָּבוֹד, שְׂבַע שְׂמָחוֹת אֶת־פָּנֶיךָ, נְעִימוֹת בִּימִינְךָ
נֶצַח. אָמֵן.

May God remember the soul of my husband who has gone to his
eternal home. In loving testimony to his life I pledge charity to
help perpetuate ideals important to him. Through such deeds, and
through prayer and memory, is his soul bound up in the bond of
life. Love is as strong as death; deep bonds of love are indissoluble.
The memory of our companionship and love overcomes loneliness,
for all that we shared still endures. May he rest forever in dignity
and peace. Amen.

In memory of a wife:

יִזְכֹּר אֱלֹהִים נִשְׁמַת אִשְׁתִּי שֶׁהָלְכָה לְעוֹלָמָהּ. הִנְנִי נוֹדֵר
צְדָקָה בְּעַד הַזְכָּרַת נִשְׁמָתָהּ. אָנָּא תְּהִי נַפְשָׁהּ צְרוּרָה בִּצְרוֹר
הַחַיִּים וּתְהִי מְנוּחָתָהּ כָּבוֹד, שֹׂבַע שְׂמָחוֹת אֶת־פָּנֶיךָ, נְעִימוֹת
בִּימִינְךָ נֶצַח. אָמֵן.

May God remember the soul of my wife who has gone to her
eternal home. In loving testimony to her life I pledge charity to
help perpetuate ideals important to her. Through such deeds, and
through prayer and memory, is her soul bound up in the bond of
life. Love is as strong as death; deep bonds of love are indissoluble.
The memory of our companionship and love overcomes loneliness,
for all that we shared still endures. May she rest forever in dignity
and peace. Amen.

In memory of a son/brother:

יִזְכֹּר אֱלֹהִים נִשְׁמַת בְּנִי הָאָהוּב מַחְמַד עֵינַי שֶׁהָלַךְ לְעוֹלָמוֹ.
הִנְנִי נוֹדֵר (נוֹדֶרֶת) צְדָקָה בְּעַד הַזְכָּרַת נִשְׁמָתוֹ. אָנָּא תְּהִי
נַפְשׁוֹ צְרוּרָה בִּצְרוֹר הַחַיִּים וּתְהִי מְנוּחָתוֹ כָּבוֹד, שֹׂבַע
שְׂמָחוֹת אֶת־פָּנֶיךָ, נְעִימוֹת בִּימִינְךָ נֶצַח. אָמֵן.

May God remember the soul of my beloved son/brother who has
gone to his eternal home. In loving testimony to his life I pledge
charity to help perpetuate ideals important to him. Through such
deeds, and through prayer and memory, is his soul bound up in
the bond of life. I am grateful for the sweetness of his life and for
what he did accomplish. May he rest forever in dignity and peace.
Amen.

In memory of a daughter or a sister:

יִזְכֹּר אֱלֹהִים נִשְׁמַת בִּתִּי הָאֲהוּבָה מַחְמַד עֵינַי שֶׁהָלְכָה לְעוֹלָמָהּ. הִנְנִי נוֹדֵר (נוֹדֶרֶת) צְדָקָה בְּעַד הַזְכָּרַת נִשְׁמָתָהּ. אָנָּא תְּהִי נַפְשָׁהּ צְרוּרָה בִּצְרוֹר הַחַיִּים וּתְהִי מְנוּחָתָהּ כָּבוֹד, שֹׂבַע שְׂמָחוֹת אֶת־פָּנֶיךָ, נְעִימוֹת בִּימִינְךָ נֶצַח. אָמֵן.

May God remember the soul of my beloved daughter/sister who has gone to her eternal home. In loving testimony to her life I pledge charity to help perpetuate ideals important to her. Through such deeds, and through prayer and memory, is her soul bound up in the bond of life. I am grateful for the sweetness of her life and for what she did accomplish. May she rest forever in dignity and peace. Amen.

In memory of other relatives and friends:

יִזְכֹּר אֱלֹהִים נִשְׁמוֹת קְרוֹבַי וְרֵעַי שֶׁהָלְכוּ לְעוֹלָמָם. הִנְנִי נוֹדֵר (נוֹדֶרֶת) צְדָקָה בְּעַד הַזְכָּרַת נִשְׁמוֹתֵיהֶם. אָנָּא תִּהְיֶינָה נַפְשׁוֹתֵיהֶם צְרוּרוֹת בִּצְרוֹר הַחַיִּים וּתְהִי מְנוּחָתָם כָּבוֹד, שֹׂבַע שְׂמָחוֹת אֶת־פָּנֶיךָ, נְעִימוֹת בִּימִינְךָ נֶצַח. אָמֵן.

May God remember the soul of ＿＿＿＿＿＿＿＿ and of all relatives and friends who have gone to their eternal home. In loving testimony to their lives I pledge charity to help perpetuate ideals important to them. Through such deeds, and through prayer and memory, are their souls bound up in the bond of life. May these moments of meditation strengthen the ties that link me to their memory. May they rest forever in dignity and peace. Amen.

Yahrzeit Diary

Yahrzeit
Anniversary of the Day of Death

Name_____

Hebrew name_____

Date_____

Hebrew date_____

Name_____

Hebrew name_____

Date_____

Hebrew date_____

Name_____

Hebrew name_____

Date_____

Hebrew date_____

Name_____

Hebrew name_____

Date_____

Hebrew date_____

Name_____

Hebrew name_____

Date_____

Hebrew date_____

Yahrzeit Diary

Yahrzeit
Anniversary of the Day of Death

Name_____

Hebrew name_____

Date_____

Hebrew date_____

Name_____

Hebrew name_____

Date_____

Hebrew date_____

Name_____

Hebrew name_____

Date_____

Hebrew date_____

Name_____

Hebrew name_____

Date_____

Hebrew date_____

Name_____

Hebrew name_____

Date_____

Hebrew date_____

READING A TOMBSTONE

Reading a Tombstone

The source:

וַיַּצֵּב יַעֲקֹב מַצֵּבָה עַל־קְבֻרָתָהּ הִוא מַצֶּבֶת קְבֻרַת־רָחֵל עַד־
הַיּוֹם:

"Over her grave Jacob set up a pillar. It is the pillar at Rachel's grave to this day" (Gen. 35:20).

What you need to know:

1. It is customary to erect a tombstone on the grave of the deceased.

2. There is no uniform practice with regard to the inscription on a stone. The stone today will often include the deceased's name in both Hebrew and English. In addition, it might also include dates of birth and death, sometimes in English and Hebrew as well.

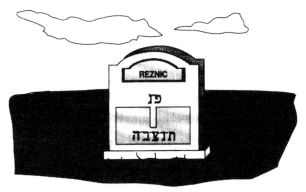

3. The Ashkenazic practice is to place the Hebrew letters פ׳נ, which stands for *po nitman*, meaning "here lies," in front of the Hebrew name of a deceased individual. The Sephardic custom is to place the Hebrew letters מ׳ק, which stands for *matzevet kevurat*, meaning "the tombstone of the grave."

פֹּה נִטְמָן
מַצֶּבֶת
קְבוּרַת

4. Many tombstones have the Hebrew letters ה'צ'ב'נ'ת. This stands for *tehe nishmato tzerurah bitzror hachayim*, which means, "may his soul be bound in the bond of eternal life."

5. Some tombstones have pictorial Jewish symbols on them. Here are eight of the more common ones:

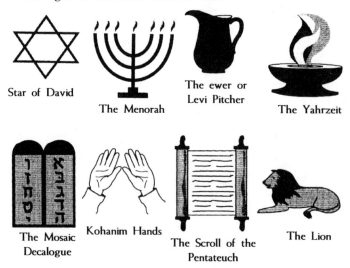

Star of David

The Menorah

The ewer or Levi Pitcher

The Yahrzeit

The Mosaic Decalogue

Kohanim Hands

The Scroll of the Pentateuch

The Lion

Things to remember:

1. A cemetery is a sacred environment. Respect it ... and the memory of those who are buried there.
2. While a cemetery is like a park, it is no playground.

Key words and phrases:

Bet chaim בֵּית חַיִּים. Euphemism for "cemetery," literally "house of life."

Bet kevarot בֵּית קְבָרוֹת. Hebrew word for "cemetery"; alternatively, *bet chaim*, "house of life."

Matzevah מַצֵּיבָה. Hebrew word for "gravestone."

Unveiling. Consecration of a tombstone, usually occurring within a calendar year of a person's death.

GLOSSARY OF TERMS

Alav Hashalom: Literally, 'peace be upon him,' A phrase used when the name of the departed is mentioned.

Aleha Hashalom: Peace be upon her.

Aninut: The status of mourning between the time of death and the burial.

Aron: Coffin.

Ashkenazim: Jews whose ancestry comes from central and Eastern Europe.

Avelim: Mourners

Baruch Dayan Emet: Literally, "Praised are You, the True Judge," recited when one learns of another's death.

Bet Olam: Literally, "eternal house", the term used for cemetery.

Bikkur Holim: Visiting the sick

Dybbuk: Literally, a clinging soul, referring to the soul of a sinner that attaches itself to a living body.

El Malei Rahamim: Literally, God, full of compassion, it is the memorial prayer for the deceased asking that the soul rest in peace.

Gan Eden: Garden of Eden.

Gehinnom: Hell, the netherworld.

Gilgul: Transmigration of the soul.

Hazkarat Neshamot: Memorial Services

Hesped: Eulogy

Kaddish Yatom: Mourner's Kaddish, recited the first year after interment.

Kevod Hamet: Honoring the deceased.

Kriah: Rending of the garment.

Levayat Hamet: The mitzvah of accompanying the dead to the grave, by way of funeral or interment.

Matzevah: Tombstone.

Olam Haba: World to come.

Onen: A mourner awaiting the burial of his or her loved one.

Po Nikbar: "Here lies buried", usually found on the headstone of a deceased person.

Sheol: The netherworld of the grave.

Shiva: Literally "seven", it refers to the seven days of mourning.

Shloshim: Thirty day period of mourning following interment.

Tachrichim: Shrouds for the dead.

Vidui: Confessional prayer.

Yahrzeit: Anniversary of the death.

Zichrono Levracha: Of blessed memory, used when speaking of the deceased; idiomatic equivalent of "may he rest in the peace."

FOR FURTHER READING

Gillman, Neil. *The Death of Death: Resurrection and Immortality in Jewish Thought.* Woodstock, VT: Jewish Lights, 1997.

Goldstein, Sidney. *Suicide in Rabbinic Literature.* Hoboken, NJ: Ktav Publishers, 1989.

Goodman, Arnold. *A Plain Pine Box.* New York: Ktav Publishers, 1981.

Greenberg, Sidney. *A Treasury of Comfort.* North Hollywood, CA: Wilshire Book Company, 1954.

Grollman, Earl A. Ed. *Explaining Death to Children.* Boston: Beacon Press, 1967.

————. *Straight Talk about Death for Teenagers* Boston: Beacon Press, 1993.

Kay, Alan A. *A Jewish Book of Comfort for Mourners.* Northvale, NJ: Jason Aronson, 1993.

Klein, Isaac. *A Time to be Born, A Time to Die.* New York: United Synagogue Department of Youth, 1976.

Lamm, Maurice. *The Jewish Way in Death and Mourning.* New York: Jonathan David, 1969.

Levine, Aaron. *To Comfort the Bereaved.* Northvale, NJ: Jason Aronson, 1994.

Rabinowicz, Tzvi. *A Guide to Life: Jewish Laws and Customs of Mourning.* Northvale, NJ: Jason Aronson, 1989.

Raphael, Simcha Paull. *Jewish Views of the Afterlife.* Northvale, NJ: Jason Aronson, 1996.

Riemer, Jack. Ed. *Jewish Reflections on Death.* New York: Schocken Books, 1976.

Riemer, Jack and Stampfer, Nathaniel. *So that Your Values Live On.* Woodstock, VT: Jewish Lights, 1991.

Sonsino Rifat, and Syme, Daniel B. *What Happens After I Die.* New York: U.A.H.C., 1990.

Spiro, Jack D. *A Time to Mourn.* New York: Bloch Publishing, 1967.

Wolfson, Ron. *A Time to Mourn A Time to Comfort.* New York: Federation of Jewish Men's Clubs, 1992.

INDEX

resurrection and, 55–56
sacredness of, 1–2
Bones, transporting of, 64–65
Bowel diseases, visiting sufferers
  of, 8
"Brit milah," 33
Brothers, yizkor remembrance
  prayer for, 127
Buber, Martin, 58
Burial(s)
  for amputated limbs, 47
  attendance by children, 54
  democratic treatment of the
    dead in, 66
  is a religious obligation, 24,
    62–63
  Jewish, 23–25
  of Moses, 95
  non-Jewish, 22–23
  of Persians, 62–63
  rabbinic sayings and stories on,
    61–70
  of a righteous person next to
    a wicked one, 65
  Sephardic, 25
  should be on the day of death,
    62
  simplicity of, 3–4, 66
Burial garments, 4, 16, 66
Burial society, 15. See also "Hevra
  kaddisha"

Candles
  in shiva observance, 29
  in yahrzeit customs, 38
  in yizkor services, 40
Caring committee. See Burial
  society; "Hevra kaddisha"
Caskets, 17–18
Catholicism. See Roman
  Catholicism
Cemeteries
  burial of ashes and, 44
  mourners leaving, 24–25, 67
  taking sanctified objects into, 65
  visiting, 37–38, 118
Cemetery rites
  Jewish, 23–25, 67
  non-Jewish, 22–23
Chanina, R., 6
Charity, memorial gifts and, 21
Children
  attendance at burials, 54
  attendance at funerals, 20–21,
    53–54
  grief and, 51, 53, 54
  as mourners, 15
  understanding death and,
    52–53
  yizkor remembrance prayers
    for, 127–128
Circumcisions, mourners and, 33
Cleansing, shiva observance and,
  29

About the Author

Rabbi Ronald Isaacs is the spiritual leader of Temple Sholom in Bridgewater, New Jersey. He received his doctorate in institutional technology from Columbia University's Teacher's College. He is the author of numerous books, including *Loving Companions: Our Jewish Wedding Album,* co-authored with Leora Isaacs. Rabbi Isaacs currently serves on the editorial board of *Shofar* magazine and is a member of the Publications Committee of the Rabbinical Assembly. He resides in New Jersey with his wife, Leora, and their children, Keren and Zachary.